Sabarimala

Sabarimala

Social History of a Temple in Kerala

Jitheesh P.M.

Introduction by Meera Velayudhan

LeftWord

First published in October 2022 by
LeftWord Books
2254/2A Shadi Khampur
New Ranjit Nagar
New Delhi 110008
INDIA

LeftWord Books and Vaam Prakashan are imprints of
Naya Rasta Publishers Pvt. Ltd.

leftword.com

ISBN 978-81-940778-3-1 (paperback)
978-81-945925-6-3 (ebook)

Printed and bound by Chaman Enterprises, Delhi

Visit website

CONTENTS

INTRODUCITON

MEERA VELAYUDHAN

In Kerala, notions of equality emerged in the early nineteenth century during the missionary period. Gender was central to the many dialogues in the social reform, anti-caste, nationalist, and communist movements in the pre-Independence era. Women and women's organizations, women's writing, and women's struggles played a distinct role in all of these movements; women came from different communities and worked together in their organizations and in these movements. This wide participation of women in Kerala's varied movements for social justice expanded the democratic dialogue and widened social democratization. The wide participation of women in people's movements was the basis of this transformation. It is what promised Malayalis equality and full citizenship, which was based on a pluralistic (*anekthvam*) and diverse social understanding. The experience of Kerala was introduced into the Constituent Assembly by three women – Annie Mascarene, Ammu Swaminadhan, and Dakshayani Velayudhan; they played a part in the framing of the Constitution and in ensuring that women's rights were enshrined in its key principles.

The gains of the past are now under severe stress. These stresses make it more difficult to confront Kerala's social and developmental challenges; this is particularly difficult for women and marginalized sections of the population. The complexities of driving a progressive agenda in this time were confounded by the worst natural disaster Kerala has yet faced – the floods of 2018, and what might as well be called economic sanctions imposed on the state government by the Central government. The post-flood reconstruction of Kerala offered an opportunity to build a new Kerala, to carry forward the gains of the past, particularly in protecting and expanding women's rights and moving towards a more egalitarian society.

However, a rational development agenda – which remains in the works – was distracted by a violent, anti-women's public agitation launched by the communal forces who opposed the Supreme Court verdict on the Sabarimala temple. This is the first time in Kerala's modern history that we have seen such a terrible and terrifying communal campaign. The Supreme Court stated that women of all ages have the right to enter Ayyappa's temple and worship there; the ban on temple entry for a section of women, aged 10 to 50 years, was effectively untouchability and therefore banned by the Constitution. It was this reasonable judgment that evoked the ire of the communal forces.

A leader of the Bharatiya Janata Party (BJP) in Kerala said that the Sabarimala verdict was a 'golden opportunity' for savarnas – dominant castes – to unite. These savarnas came together rapidly. The alliance combined the ancient unity of the temple Thanthris of the ex-rajas of Travancore (Pandalam) and the dominant-caste Nair Service Society (NSS) with the more modern political formations of the BJP and the fascist Rashtriya Swayamsevak Sangh (RSS); the Congress Party tagged along. This communal bloc included women as well – many from the former dominant-caste matrilineal communities, several of them educated professionals; they propagated their own social exclusion as the defence of 'tradition'. Violent threats, hate speech, caste abuse – everything that was nasty and objectionable – emerged from the communal forces led by the BJP.

This bloc of the hard Right, however, could not intimidate the rest of Kerala. A powerful popular discourse emerged around the idea of *navodhanam* – Renaissance. This discourse drew from Kerala's social reform and left history to make the argument that the Renaissance tradition of Kerala must not only be defended and strengthened, but also expanded. Large public meetings were held, with Chief Minister Pinarayi Vijayan playing a leading role. In these meetings, Pinarayi Vijayan and others explained the role of the social movements in fighting caste slavery and oppression, as well as of Sabarimala's history, and the case that went to the Supreme Court. This was one massive public seminar in Kerala's Renaissance history. Several Dalit groups and organizations, intellectuals, and other new social movements – who had their own independent view – nonetheless gave critical support to the Left Democratic Front government. Broad cultural platforms were formed under the theme of 'We the People', leading to several public events that focused on the Constitution and on women's constitutional rights.

The most visible part of the protest was the Vanitha Mathil (Women's Wall) that was constructed on 1 January 2019 by thousands of women and men from one end of Kerala to the other. This Wall – a symbol of the resoluteness of the Renaissance tradition – was built by mobilizations and campaigns at the local panchayat (village council) level; it drew women leaders from diverse collectives and community organizations like Kudumbasree, Ayalkoottam, Anganwadis, and so on. The anti-caste campaign at the root of the struggle appealed to the defence and expansion of women's constitutional rights; this struck a chord amongst a wide section of women, who took to the streets to build the Wall. For the first time since the 2018 floods, women came out in public and said, 'We have an opinion and have something to say on what is going on and on what impacts us the most'. The democratic decentralization process – despite its weaknesses – had found deep roots in Kerala; the broad-based women's leadership carried forward the possibility of radical transformation of an ongoing political process in this time of crisis. At stake was the possibility of transforming the patriarchal political culture.

The Sabarimala case is now in danger of reversal. The Court had said in September 2018 that women of all age groups could enter the temple. Now, there is a suggestion that this might not stand, which would then undermine the basic tenets of the Constitution – in particular, women's constitutional rights. There is a need to be vigilant.

This book, by a young scholar and journalist, provides one perspective on the events that followed the landmark Court judgment, and on the history of Sabarimala. It draws on a variety of sources and provides a rich story. No doubt, this book will be followed by other interpretations. A well documented book such as this one will, hopefully, generate more informed debates in the tradition of Kerala's Renaissance.

PART 1

WOMEN IN SABARIMALA: KERALA RENAISSANCE AND THE REVIVALIST CHALLENGE

On 28 September 2018, the Constitution bench of the Supreme Court of India, in a landmark judgment, allowed women of all ages to enter the Sabarimala temple in Kerala.

The Supreme Court carefully examined the Kerala Hindu Places of Public Worship (Authorization of Entry) Rules of 1965. These rules were formulated on the basis of the laws set down by the Madras Temple Entry Authorization Act of 1947. Rule 3 of the 'authorization of entry' rules provides a list of people who can be barred from entry into the temple. These include non-Hindus, 'drunken or disorderly persons', 'persons suffering from any loathsome or contagious disease' and 'persons under pollution arising out of birth or death in their families'. Then comes the important sub-rule, 3(b):

> Women at such time during which they are not by custom and usage allowed to enter a place of public worship.

In 1955 and 1956, the Travancore Devaswom Board (TDB) issued notifications that prevented women between the ages of ten and fifty from entering the temple.[1] The precise notification read:

As Sabarimala Ayyappa is *Nithya Brahmachari* [celibate], women between the 10–50 age group are not allowed to enter Sabarimala. Such women who try to enter Sabarimala will be prevented by authorities.

The Supreme Court rejected these arguments. The Indian

[1] The Travancore Devaswom Board, an autonomous body constituted under the Travancore-Cochin Hindu Religious Institutions Act, 1950, looks after 1,248 temples of the erstwhile princely state of Travancore formerly under the care of the ruler of Travancore. The Sabarimala temple is one of these.

Constitution (1950) and the Protection of Civil Rights Act (1955) had already made clear that such restrictions, based on any social distinction (particularly on questions of untouchability), are impermissible.

This indicates that some forms of exclusion had a longer history at Sabarimala that pre-date the 1991 Kerala High Court judgment (discussed below). But we don't have evidence to say that these existed since 'time immemorial'; these were often executive orders. And it is true that even after these orders, women of said age used to visit Sabarimala. In 1986, as part of the shooting of the Tamil film *Nambinar Keduvathillai*, female actresses under the age of 50 entered the premises. Evidence of the queen of Travancore visiting the temple is produced in the latter part of this book. Incidents of women of menstruating age visiting the temple in the 1980s are well known; they ultimately resulted in the 1991 case.

Had it been the case that banning women's entry was part of an essential practice, then such instances would certainly have been infrequent. Looking at its history, however, the Supreme Court did not consider the ban an 'essential practice' and hence covered under Article 26, which provides a constitutional framework that upholds the principle of equality and how it should respond to beliefs that compromise these rights of a section of the people.

In 1991, the Kerala High Court legalized the ban set by the TDB and the Sabarimala priests. This ban was based on the concept of pollution. Only unpolluted people, it is said, can be part of the 41-day pilgrimage and visit the Sabarimala temple. Those 41 days are a 'period of penance' (*vratham*), said the High Court judgment in 1991. 'Women of the age group

10 to 50,' said the Kerala High Court, 'will not be in a position to observe *vratham* continuously for a period of 41 days due to physiological reasons.'[2] What the Court meant is that it is more than likely that women would menstruate during the 41-day period, and since menstruation is a form of pollution in the orthodox Hindu framework, women simply cannot be unpolluted. The Supreme Court rejected this verdict. The Supreme Court bench argued that using menstruation as a barrier to entry was tantamount to considering women untouchable, and since the Constitution bans untouchability, this practice must also be banished from Indian society. The Court's clarity is worth quotation:

> Prejudice against women based on notions of impurity and pollution associated with menstruation is a symbol of exclusion. The social exclusion of women based on menstrual status is a form of untouchability, which is an anathema to constitutional values.
>
> The court must decline to grant constitutional legitimacy to practices that derogate from the dignity of women and their entitlement to an equal citizenship.[3,4]

The Supreme Court did not shy away from the implications of its verdict for broader questions of gender justice. 'We have no hesitation in saying that such an exclusionary practice

[2] S. Mahendran v. The Secretary, Travancore Devaswom Board, Thiruvananthapuram. Read more: https://indiankanoon.org/doc/1915943/

[3] Indian Young Lawyers Association & Ors vs The State of Kerala & Ors. Read here: https://main.sci.gov.in/supremecourt/2006/18956/18956_2006_Judgement_28-Sep-2018.pdf p.164.

[4] Ibid., p.116.

violates the right of women to visit and enter a temple to freely practice the Hindu religion and to exhibit her [sic] devotion towards lord Ayyappa. The denial of this right to women significantly denudes them of their right to worship.'[5]

'Patriarchy in religion cannot be permitted to trump over elements of pure devotion borne out of faith and the freedom to practice and profess one's religion,' said Chief Justice Dipak Misra.

The Supreme Court verdict came on the heels of the most devastating natural disaster the state has faced in a century. According to government sources, the state received an excess of 96 per cent rainfall from 1 to 30 August 2018 and 33 per cent during the entire monsoon period till the end of August. While 3,415,937 people were evacuated to 12,253 camps across the state, several hundred people lost their lives, and thousands of homes were fully destroyed.[6] According to official data, total recovery needs were estimated at 31,000 crore rupees (USD 4.4 billion).[7] The intangible losses were greater.

Immediately after the Supreme Court verdict on Sabarimala, the Left Democratic Front (LDF) government in Kerala announced that it would not file any review petition against the judgment. The government said that it would make necessary arrangements for any woman who wished to visit the Sabarimala temple as per the instructions of the Supreme Court. A democratic government has a constitutional

[5] Ibid., p. 64.

[6] *Additional Memorandum. Kerala Floods – 2018*, Government of Kerala, 2018.

[7] *Kerala. Post Disaster Needs Assessment: Floods and Landslides – August 2018*, Government of Kerala, October 2018.

obligation to follow a Supreme Court judgment and to uphold the rule of law.[8] The Kerala government did not stop there and has taken the position that it has the responsibility to champion the cause of gender justice and women's equality against the compulsions of patriarchy and other forms of archaic brutality.

All political parties outside the ruling LDF – the BJP in particular, but including the Indian National Congress, the Indian Union Muslim League (IUML), Kerala Congress (M), Kerala Congress (J), Bharath Dharma Jana Sena and even the Revolutionary Socialist Party Kerala Unit – took a position against the Supreme Court judgement and in defence of the restrictions on women's entry. They attacked the government headed by Pinarayi Vijayan as a force that wanted to change the traditional attitude towards the Sabarimala pilgrimage, leaving the Supreme Court verdict out of the picture. These political forces let loose an unprecedented level of street protests, and some even engaged in vandalism. Verbal attacks, social media attacks, and even physical attacks against women who favoured the verdict were fierce. Sangh Parivar-led right-wing groups were in the forefront of agitations that besieged Kerala.

The attack on the LDF government for its stand on the Sabarimala verdict came just as Kerala was recovering from the flood. The state government and social forces immediately recognized the tragedy and devastation and devoted themselves to rebuilding and reconstruction. Kerala displayed great unity,

[8] According to Article 129 of the Constitution, the Supreme Court 'shall have . . . the power to punish for contempt of itself'. Also, Article 142(2) and the Contempt of Courts Act, 1971, confer on the Supreme Court powers to enforce its decisions and punish those who fail to abide by them.

irrespective of caste and religion, as various sections of the public cooperated to rescue and evacuate those most severely impacted by the flood. As the waters receded, the stature of the LDF government rose.

It was against this background that the BJP, the Congress, and their allies wielded the issue of Sabarimala. The Supreme Court judgment came as an opportunity for both the Congress and the Bharatiya Janata Party (whose state president even called it a 'golden chance' for the party to target the Left). While the Congress projected the disaster as mainly man-made – the release of water from dams – with respect to Sabarimala, it took a leading role in opposing women's entry. It was a big shift from its earlier, wider social base among different communities to a more pronounced upper-caste-led agenda. It coincided with the BJP agenda. The political motives of the parties ruptured the unity of Malayalis, diverting attention from concrete acts of solidarity to ameliorating human tragedy towards abstract notions of belief and custom. What characterized the reaction of political forces opposing the Supreme Court was – as Prabhat Patnaik put it – the 'promotion of unreason, prioritization of faith over rational discourse, a cultivation of disdain for evidence, and even for internal consistency of argumentation'.[9]

A comment by historian K.N. Ganesh is worth quoting in this context:

> The patriarchal gaze on a woman in the name of checking whether she is of menstruating age or not violated all

[9] Prabhat Patnaik, 'Shadow of Fascism', *Frontline*, 12 April 2019.

> democratic norms and concepts of women's equality. The Sabarimala issue shows that the hard-gained humanistic achievements of Kerala society are in real danger.[10]

Society was more or less split into two camps. The first political camp, represented by the Left, believed in women's rights in Sabarimala and supported the Supreme Court verdict. The second camp, represented by the BJP and its allies, and the United Democratic Front (UDF), took a position against the verdict and for maintaining the custom. While others in the second camp, represented by the Sangh Parivar and the orthodoxy, only took a position against the verdict. Some of the famous liberals in the state were, by and large, assimilated into the camp of the Right on this issue. There was no room to bridge the gap. The issue that divided society into these camps was central to belief systems and attitudes to fundamental questions of culture and belief. The progressive camp, supporting the Supreme Court judgement, faced the challenge of frenzied protests by launching a counter-mobilization and a counter-narrative. It had to inspire millions of women and men in Kerala to strengthen their resolve on these issues.

This counter-narrative was formulated by invoking the renaissance tradition of Kerala, the rich legacy of social reforms, and heroic anti-caste struggles. The Sabarimala agitation was presented before millions as a social counterrevolution. Politicians, intellectuals, and writers who believed in the principles of rationality, secularism, and gender sensitivity invoked this past widely to make people conscious of and

[10] An interview with K.N. Ganesh. Available here: https://www.youtube.com/watch?v=eCES0i2HNjg&feature=youtube , last accessed 12 March 2020.

recall the events and processes that shaped what they are today. Pinarayi Vijayan played a pivotal role in building this narrative. In his widely attended public meetings, he explained to the common masses the history of the litigation around Sabarimala, linking it with anti-caste movements of the past and the renaissance, *navodhanam*, and how these were crucial to building a new Kerala, particularly after disaster.

In his speech on 16 October 2018 at Thiruvananthapuram Vijayan said:

> Our great legacy is that of our renaissance. Our society is based on that legacy of renaissance. The renaissance movement came up under the leadership of Sree Narayana Guru, Chattambi Swamikal, Ayyankali, and so on. That is how this land, which Swami Vivekananda once called a lunatic asylum, transformed itself into a model for the entire country, with its commitment to secularism and uprooting casteism.
>
> In some places in our country, there was the practice of human sacrifice. It was later changed to animal sacrifice. Later, even that changed to symbolic sacrifice, using a red liquid made of turmeric, quicklime, and so on. These are all changes in customs. So, many such changes have occurred in our country, in our state. A custom is a traditional practice that would change from time to time. A custom that is common at one point of time may not be there at a later time . . . There are various struggles that happened in our land.
>
> The Kerala that we see today was born through those struggles. The struggles to break the stone necklaces that

> Dalit women had to wear for others to identify them. The struggle for everybody to sit together in schools to study. The struggle to allow everybody to enter jobs after studies. The struggle to win the freedom to use public roads. The struggle to win the right to enter temples and worship. We should remember that the Kerala we see today was built through various such struggles.

Vijayan played a key role in the alliances forged with community and caste groups that supported the Supreme Court verdict. Engaging with caste and bringing the understanding of the necessity for it into the political movement was a complex task. Punnala Sreekumar, general secretary of the Kerala Pulayar Maha Sabha (KPMS), was among the first to support the court's verdict. Vellappally Natesan, general secretary of the Sree Narayana Dharma Paripalana Yogam (SNDP Yogam), said that there was a need for all secular sections to come together. The formation of a larger committee of such groups, although critiqued by some sections which supported the Supreme Court verdict, in fact, checked the momentum of the BJP-led agitation and helped to provide a wider base of support for the LDF government's stand and actions around the verdict on Sabarimala.

First, the state government had to follow its constitutional duty to maintain law and order through the use of state machinery. The acts of vandalism and violence by agitators faced strong measures from the state government. The chief minister said on many occasions:

> Government would not be cowed by threats and

> intimidation. Violence is violence and the government will take strong measures to curb it. In other states, when RSS unleash violence, no action is taken and even those who commit daylight murders are not brought to book. Such people will not get protection in Kerala.[11]

The government's firm hand prevented social chaos and guided the state to relative normalcy. In many parts of the country, on different occasions, the inaction or the complicity of government machinery has often aggravated violent situations, plunging society into dangerous anarchy.

In contrast, in Kerala, by 6 January 2019, after two women successfully entered the Sabarimala temple on 2 January, the Kerala police arrested 6,711 right-wing provocateurs and assailants as they took to the streets to provoke violence. The police registered cases against 2,182 people and remanded 894 of them. The state returned to normalcy in a speedy fashion. The police were tasked with providing security to women who wanted to trek to Sabarimala, including the two women who entered the temple.

Outside the legal and constitutional duties of the government, left forces worked alongside other social forces to galvanize public support for the cause of gender justice. These public support programmes were built around the concept of the Kerala Renaissance – the entire tradition of social reform that came out of the nineteenth century into the twenty-first century. The ideas of the Renaissance and the Constitution framed the counter-narrative of all those

[11] *The Asian Age*, 7 January 2019.

who favoured the Supreme Court judgement. In November 2018, the government decided to celebrate the eighty-second anniversary of the historic temple entry proclamation of 1936. This proclamation allowed 'untouchable' castes into temples controlled by the Travancore Kingdom. It was not just because of the 'open mindednesses' of the royal family. Agitations and struggles that preceded the proclamation had pushed them to do it. Some historians argue that fear of conversion by the oppressed castes to other religions also helped bring about the temple entry proclamation. The celebration of the eighty-second anniversary evoked the Renaissance tradition's antipathy to social hierarchy based on norms of caste. The Kerala State Assembly and the Kerala Literacy Mission organized Constitution protection yathras (processions) from Kasaragod to Thiruvananthapuram to instil the values of the Constitution in the people.

The orthodoxy and groups who protested, opposing the verdict, struggled hard to present rational arguments. Their main contention centred around the idea of 'custom'. They knew that it would be courting disaster to have older men speak against women's entry into Sabarimala. Which is why they mobilized women to agitate against the Supreme Court verdict and speak in favour of archaic customs. Women came out in large numbers for the Namajapa Gosha Yathras, launched by the orthodox sections against the verdict.

In response, left forces took to the streets with massive mobilizations. LDF held public meetings across the state, while the communist parties launched prolonged campaigns to explain their position. They were joined by mass organizations like the Democratic Youth Federation of India (DYFI), the

All India Youth Federation, the Progressive Arts & Literary Organization, the All-India Democratic Women's Association (AIDWA), the Students' Federation of India (SFI), the All India Students' Federation (AISF), etc. They called their gatherings *Navodhana Sadhasukal* or 'Renaissance Gatherings' and held them across the state.

The organizational strength and deep base of the Left among the working-class and other sections of society helped them mobilize people, including a large number of women, to explain their position. The enthusiastic participation in the 'Women's Wall' and the strong stand against the violence perpetuated by hard-right organizations proved how deep an organic link with the common masses the campaigns had, as well as with the educational function of making women aware of the danger they face in violent agitations.

Beneath the question of the Supreme Court verdict lies the deeper cultural issue of pollution. The traditional belief of the orthodoxy was that people who are 'polluted' – menstruating women and all 'untouchables' – should not be allowed into temples. There is a direct link between these two. That is why the Left, progressive women's groups, Dalit, and tribal groups fought against the ideology of patriarchy and the view that menstruation makes one impure. They looked back at the social reformer and Dalit icon Ayyankali's *Villuvandi Yathra*, a historic protest in 1893 for the rights of Dalits to walk on public roads.[12] At Kochi, groups held an *Aarpo Arthavam* ('Hurray Menstruation') rally against the idea of menstruation as pollution. Social media campaigns with the hashtag

[12] *The News Minute*, 14 December 2018.

#WomenNotImpure got considerable visibility. A Dalit and Adivasi women's Villuvandi Yathra was also organized, drawing wider sections of women.

THE LEGAL HISTORY – DIFFERING APPROACHES

The historic judgment by the Indian Supreme Court came after many years of legal battles. In 2006, the Indian Young Lawyers Association filed a public interest litigation in the Court on the grounds that the rule in Sabarimala violated the freedom to worship listed in Article 25 of the Indian Constitution. The next year, in November 2007, the Left Democratic Front government, headed by Chief Minister V.S. Achuthanandan, filed an affidavit supporting the demand for the entry of women of menstruation age to Sabarimala.

The process moved slowly forward, but on 6 February 2016 the UDF government filed an affidavit in court that banning entry of women of menstruation age in historic Sabarimala is a 'matter of religion' and it was duty-bound to 'protect the right to practice [their] religion of these devotees'. What they meant was that the restriction should not be lifted.

The new LDF government, led by Pinarayi Vijayan, on 7 November 2016 filed a new affidavit in the Supreme Court, stating that it favoured the entry of women of all ages into the temple. This position of the government was crucial for the eventual court verdict.

The difference between the principles of the Left (represented by the Left Democratic Front) and the Right (represented by the United Democratic Front and National

Democratic Alliance) is stark. It becomes starker once the Supreme Court delivered its verdict.

The landmark judgment was welcomed by progressive sections of the society – the women's rights movement, the Left, and millions who valued women's equality – who saw it as a step forward in the direction of women's equality. Chief Minister Pinarayi Vijayan said, 'The government will go by the Supreme Court order. We have to execute the order. The government will not file [a] review petition'. In other words, the government would not contest the Court's decision.[13] In an interview with the present author, the chief minister said:

> [The] nation's constitution is supreme and above all the customs and beliefs. In the verdict, the Supreme Court has clearly spelled out that any violation of the fundamental rights guaranteed by our Constitution can't be allowed. All governments [that] come to power based on constitutional principles are obliged to uphold the Constitution as supreme.[14]

Immediately following the Supreme Court verdict, conservative social groups openly articulated their displeasure at the judgement. They were joined by the Sangh Parivar groups, who had long pushed for a homogenous, Brahminical interpretation of the rituals at Sabarimala, although these were contested by tribal groups such as Mala Araya. In the name of protecting the faith and custom at Sabarimala, these various groups pushed an agenda against lifting the ban on the entry

[13] *The Hindu*, 3 October 2018.

[14] *The Hindu*, 7 March 2019.

of women of menstruating age to Sabarimala. The Sabarimala temple Thanthri even quoted the *Sankara Smriti* – which said that menstruating women cannot brush their teeth, take a bath, or apply kohl on their eyes – and made clear that this was the book they followed. The rights and powers of the thanthri thus came into question as well.

The Kerala government and left parties had already identified menstruation as a health issue in the public sphere and in policy by initiating programmes to provide free sanitary napkins in schools. This was widely appreciated by girls and young women.

The main contention behind the agitation was that the custom of restriction of women in Sabarimala is ancient, and that the Supreme Court's verdict is a transgression of the Right to religion and religious freedom – a fundamental right guaranteed by the Constitution. The idea that restriction of women is 'tradition', had been cemented into the arguments not only of the orthodoxy but also among politicians such as Shashi Tharoor. However, there is ample evidence to show that the ban on women's entry into the temple is not ancient and that it dates back, strictly, to the Kerala High Court verdict of 1991. In the second part of this book, evidence of women of menstruation age entering Sabarimala before 1991 is discussed.

Oppressed and Dominant

Who led the agitations against the Supreme Court verdict? The groups that led the agitation came from the orthodox sections of society, and politically various Sangh Parivar groups and UDF took the lead. They included the Nair Service Society (NSS), the Akhila Bharatha Ayyappa Seva Sangham (ABASS), the Kerala Brahmana Sabha, the Ayyappa Dharma Sena, the former Pandalam royal family, the Thazhamon family (consisting of the chief priests of Sabarimala), etc. Two days after the Supreme Court judgment, Rahul Easwar – an activist in the Ayyappa Dharma Sena and a member of the Thazhamon family – not only expressed his displeasure at the verdict, but openly threatened women. Those women who would try and enter Sabarimala, he said, could only do so by 'stamping on the chests of devotees'. Protests, he said, 'would be organized against their entry across the state'. Indeed, they organized these agitations which were revivalist in character.

NSS, a powerful dominant caste organization, was at the forefront of these agitations. It was the first to challenge the Supreme Court verdict and it was the first on the streets. They protested on the streets as the Namajapa Gosha Yathra. The NSS's leadership sent a firm message to all its *karayogams* (units) to fill the streets.[15] The Nair Service Society and the Sangh Parivar channeled the fear amongst sections of the dominant-caste population that their superiority was being challenged. Historian Rajan Gurukkal writes:

> Culturally uprooted masses clap their hands and shout *saranam* with militant fervour to protect the Ayyappa 'tradition'. It is actually the anxiety of losing their Savarna caste status, rank, and identity that brings them out on the streets.[16]

[15] *The New Indian Express*, 14 October 2018.

[16] Rajan Gurukkal, 'Sabarimala: The Past and Present', *The Indian Express*, 22

Many oppressed-caste organizations and leaders immediately understood that the actions of these protesting groups were not a principled defence of 'tradition' but to maintain their dominant status and interests. The SNDP Yogam – a caste organization of Ezhavas – weakened the protests. The general secretary of SNDP Yogam, Vellappally Natesan, said at the start of the agitation that the protesters did not represent all Hindus:

> Those who came out for the protest say that they represent the entire Hindu community. But how can they claim that when the Ezhavas, which constitute around 28 per cent of the Hindus in Kerala, are not part of the protests, neither are scheduled castes and scheduled tribes.

'The attitude that lower castes should take orders from the upper castes,' Natesan said, 'is not appropriate'. Punnala Sreekumar, the general secretary of the Kerala Pulayar Maha Sabha, concurred. The protesters, Sreekumar said, 'are trying to protect upper-caste domination, which is losing its last frontier.' Dalit activist Sunny M. Kapikad stated that:

> The basic problem lies in the fear that Sabarimala would become a public space with the verdict, and by this, the Thantri family will lose dominance. In fact, the dominant caste people are afraid that once the judgement is executed, people from the lower castes, would be appointed as priests . . . .[17]

December 2018.

[17] *The News Minute*, 12 October 2018.

'The verdict is the continuation of the reformation movements [begun] by Sree Narayana Guru,' said Sreekumar, making the case that this is a long fight for a progressive society in Kerala. 'Our society failed to take forward the ideological fight of Narayana Guru and hence a court judgment was needed for that.'[18] The Adivasi leader C.K. Janu agreed with Sreekumar. 'The Supreme Court verdict is in keeping with the idea of gender equality, guaranteed by the Constitution. This idea of the Constitution is being challenged on the streets. Challenging the Constitution on the streets would lead to anarchy', she said.[19] The Adivasi Gothra Maha Sabha welcomed the Supreme Court verdict.

These groups and leaders saw that the agitators did not seem to want women of all ages to enter the Sabarimala temple and to enjoy equal rights in society. The issue is not merely about temple entry. It is about equal rights. That was clear to these organizations. It was also clear that those who welcomed the Supreme Court verdict not only wanted women to be allowed to freely enter the Sabarimala temple, but they believed that women should have the fullest rights in society.

The open use of abusive caste-laden language was a major characteristic of agitations against the Supreme Court verdict. This kind of language was, to a large extent, restricted in Kerala's public sphere. These people routinely attacked Pinarayi Vijayan along caste lines. A video that went viral on social media and was constantly posted by many of the agitators showed an elderly woman from Pathanamthitta, who said that Vijayan's face should be thrashed. She used offensive casteist

[18] Ibid.

[19] *Deccan Chronicle*, 14 November 2018.

language as well. 'P. Vijayan should leave his post and return to his caste profession as a toddy tapper', said senior BJP leader N. Sivarajan. The BJP mouthpiece in Kerala – *Janmabhoomi* – ran a cartoon in its regular column *Drisakshi* (eyewitness) on the front page that alludes to Pinarayi Vijayan's background. Three people in the cartoon discuss the Sabarimala issue; one person says that the government's support for women's entry into the temple is a consequence of giving the top post in the state to a man who used to climb coconut trees. Pinarayi Vijayan's father – Koran – was a toddy tapper. This was a direct casteist slur against the Chief Minister, and due to the emerging criticism, *Janmabhoomi* sacked the cartoonist.

Renaissance vs Revivalism

Conservatives argued that 'customs are sacrosanct' and that 'tradition is age-old, hence unchangeable'. This was their argument for why women of menstruation age should not be allowed into the Sabarimala temple complex. It did not matter whether these claims were sustainable, or that the arguments were based on facts, used logic, or represented the values of modernity. Indeed, there weren't reasonable arguments defining the reaction. The nature of the resistance to women entering the Sabarimala temple is defined by their disavowal of Kerala's Renaissance process, which includes the long history of Kerala's social reform movement.

Pinarayi Vijayan saw the fight over Sabarimala as part of the long history of Kerala's social reform struggle. 'Our renaissance leaders taught us that some customs are meant to be broken', he said at the huge public meeting held in Thiruvananthapuram on 16 October 2018. During the Renaissance movement, he said, leaders such as Sree Narayana Guru, Chattambi Swamikal, and Ayyankali smashed several social customs and traditions. Narayana Guru, a non-Brahmin leader, consecrated a Siva idol in Aruvippuram in 1888. Ayyankali, born into an oppressed-caste community (the Pulayars), pushed against the hierarchical distinctions of caste society. For example, he rejected clothes traditionally associated with his caste and wore the clothing of the Nairs while he propagated the importance of education for oppressed castes. He played an important role in the Perinad Lahala, where women of oppressed castes threw away their ornaments made of stone and wood – *kallumala* – and pledged to only wear ornaments of gold and metal. Oppressed castes went on the offensive, walking on prohibited roads and entering temples. 'Swami Vivekananda said of Kerala's caste-ridden society that it was a "lunatic asylum"; it became a secular and democratic society due to the Renaissance movement. Fascistic elements wish to drag Kerala back to the "lunatic asylum"' he said.[20]

The Renaissance legacy of breaking traditions and customs, not the ritual of keeping traditions and customs intact, brought significant changes in the social life of Kerala. It propelled the state to the highest levels of the various human development indices. Many of these old traditions and customs, which developed in the pre-modern period, were brutal, and they were against the spirit of human freedom, equality, and dignity. It is worthwhile to list some of these brutalities:

[20] Available here: https://m.youtube.com/watch?v=ThcKH5AqspE& feature=youtu.be

- The 'breast tax' (*mulakkaram*) was imposed by dominant castes on Dalit and other 'lower-caste' women.
- Ban on oppressed castes to travel on particular roads.
- Ban on oppressed castes to enter temples.
- Ban on inter-marriage across castes.
- Ban on inter-dining across castes.

These were just a few of the most regressive and anti-human customs prevalent in Kerala well into the twentieth century. Such prejudices and discrimination were based on caste and gender hierarchies, and, of course, had various justification theories applied in the form of customs and traditions in religion.

In the nineteenth and twentieth centuries, protests and struggles emerged from the oppressed castes and from women against these customs and traditions. These protests and struggles were part of a wider fight against the ideological fetters of what the communist leader E.M.S. Namboodiripad called the 'Jati-Janmi-Landlord' system that existed in Kerala. This wider fight stretched from a battle over landlordism to the humiliating customs. There was genuine revolutionary zeal in these struggles:

1. Channar Revolt (1813–59)
2. Aruvippuram Consecration (1888)
3. Villuvandi agitation (1893)
4. Kallumala or stone-chain agitation (1915)
5. Misra Bhojan or community feast (1917)
6. Vaikom Satyagraha (1924)
7. Guruvayoor Satyagraha (1931–32)

These, and many other struggles, went up against one or another custom or tradition that existed in Kerala. However, these were not merely reform movements against this or that custom but were revolutionary in character – against the entire social and economic system. It was this Renaissance legacy that the chief minister referred to throughout the debate over Sabarimala. Vijayan was 'fanning the spark of hope in the past', to paraphrase the German Marxist Walter Benjamin. He fanned this spark as he was 'firmly convinced that even the dead will not be safe from the enemy if he were not victorious'.

The Sabarimala issue originated from the deep toxicity and aggressiveness of the patriarchy in Kerala's society. The unfinished agenda of Kerala's Renaissance is at the centre of this patriarchy and revivalism. It is clear that Kerala was not able to undergo a thorough modernization process. As a result of this, Kerala's society could not go beyond the entrenched values of the old rooted order, which is the enemy of Kerala's Renaissance tradition. Kerala, with a history of capitalist development integrated with colonialism, was organized on the basis of various pre-modern identities that competed with each other for educational and employment opportunities. These sharp contests are reflected in such caste organizations as the NSS – for Nairs – and the SNDP Yogam – for Ezhavas. The community consolidation among the Christian and Muslim minorities also reflects this. In the context of Kerala's modernisation, the phenomenon of community-based 'upliftment' stood in the way of forming broader class solidarity. Casteism and nostalgia for the old order find easy footing in this context.

Kerala's Renaissance did not adequately deal a blow to

ideas of gender oppression and patriarchy. Patriarchy remains dominant in Kerala's society, and provides the historical reservoir from which, and contemporary framework within which, anti-women ideas are received and reproduced. The idea that menstruation is a sign of women's impurity is key to this entire worldview. That women of a certain age range are banned from Sabarimala has everything to do with this idea of menstruation making women impure, and that impurity must not be permitted in a temple (or in other spaces). The Supreme Court judgement specifically rejected the view that considers menstruation as an impurity. These questions – unresolved by the Kerala Renaissance – remain central issues for our times.

Certainly, the power of ideology – in this case, patriarchy – was such that it galvanized large sections of women, including a large number of elite women, to protest against the Supreme Court order. They came out in large numbers for the Namajapa Gosha Yathra in October 2018. That the court's order opened up places such as Sabarimala to women and that it pushed against the idea of the impurity of women did not turn these women against what are seen to be their key traditions and customs. They protested to prevent themselves from going into Sabarimala. Women from such dominant-caste communities or 'kulin' women are not often seen at public protests in Kerala. So, their presence on the streets was twice as surprising: not only because they were protesting against ideologies that considered them impure, but that they were protesting at all. It was the first time since the Vimochana Samaram ('Liberation Struggle') of 1959 that women from the dominant castes came into the streets in such large numbers; that protest resulted in the dismissal of the E.M.S. Namboodiripad government by Prime Minister Nehru. Unfortunately, even educated women are now coming forward to say – exclude us, as it is the tradition.

The agitation against the entry of women of menstruation age into Sabarimala was conducted not only by the old feudal sections of Hindus, but also by members of the newly emergent middle-class Hindu population, irrespective of their caste background. K.N. Panikkar writes:

> Kerala has witnessed a sudden burgeoning of the lower middle class during the last two decades, whose craving for modernity has created a cultural crisis, a solution for which they sought in superstitious practices and irrational rituals.[21]

Material gains from migrant work in the Persian Gulf drove some of this cultural crisis. Sections of Kerala's Muslim community have made substantial gains in the last two decades. This is largely due to the fortunes made from migration to the Gulf, but Hindu right-wing groups have slightly succeeded in portraying this as a consequence of the appeasement of Muslims by the LDF and UDF coalitions. This kind of attitude – coupled with the idea that Hindus are in decline – sharpened the communal outlook of sections of the petit-bourgeois and middle-class Hindus. Sharpening of the communal outlook is not limited to a section of Hindus but a reality among a section of Muslims and Christians too. Such campaigns enable unity among sections of the Hindu population irrespective of caste

[21] K.N. Panikkar, 'Not merely a two-way contest', *The Hindu*, 7 April 2016.

hierarchy. (Hindu Aikyavedi State President K.P. Sasikala is the chief organizer of the Sabarimala Karma Samithi, the most important omnibus group that led the agitations against the Supreme Court verdict.)

The case of temple committees is significant in the efforts toward homogenizing. Temple committees are mushrooming in the state, where members from all castes are inducted. Earlier, the ownership and organization of Brahminical temples and execution of temple affairs rested solely with the upper castes. Gradually, with the changed social context, as a result of anti-caste struggles, it became impossible to openly discriminate against lower-caste people as such action would result in strong resistance. It seems that arithmetic also works to support such efforts. Numbers matter for the claims of being the majority. Statistics show that Hindus constitute roughly 55 per cent of the total population of the state. Out of this, the upper castes constitute much less than 20 per cent. The rest – more than 30 per cent – include the Ezhava, Viswakarma, SC, ST, and other castes, which are lower down the caste hierarchy. This arithmetic is a compelling force in the accommodation of marginalized castes. Today, people from marginalized communities and castes are increasingly inducted into the affairs of local temple management committees. Here the criteria used to induct them is the identification of being a *viswasi* (devotee). But the most important thing to take note of is that this homogenizing effort doesn't upset the hierarchical caste division. The Hindu or viswasi identity doesn't cancel your caste identity!

The reality of the temple committees, however, is that without any change in ownership and ritual traditions, the role of the newly inducted members from marginalized castes seems to be mainly that of executing temple affairs, which are ultimately determined by the Brahmin priest and the traditional authorities of the temple.

Moreover, the elites among the dominant community groups are not prepared to go out into the streets and fight. So, to give their project visibility and execute it, the dominant classes need the help of right-wing cadres at the ground level.

According to media reports, the BJP state unit issued a circular, on behalf of General Secretary A.N. Radhakrishnan, ordering their cadres to reach Sabarimala. The circular, dated 17 November, was to ensure that their activists would be there at Sabarimala to execute their planned agitation, from 18 November to 15 December from across the roughly 30 Sangh Districts in the state, each 'Sangh District' comprises three to eight constituencies.[22] It was these cadres who forcefully prevented women from entering the Sabarimala premises, taking to the streets to propel the agitation, which in many instances turned violent.

The RSS-BJP were strongly opposed to the Supreme Court verdict and its implementation. They were fully in favour of the ban on the entry of women of menstruation age into Sabarimala. Meanwhile, the BJP state president also revealed the political motives in their stand. Sreedharan Pillai, then the Kerala unit president of BJP, addressed BJP cadres at a Yuva Morcha meeting in 2018. He told them, 'Sabarimala is a puzzle. We cannot expect it to move along a fixed-line. But we have put forward an agenda, and others are gradually falling for it.

[22] *Mathrubhumi*, 19 November 2018.

It is a golden chance'.[23] It was a 'golden chance' to do two things – to promote their political and ideological agenda across Kerala and to use the agitation to build up the BJP's options for the 2019 Lok Sabha election. To do both, the Sangh Parivar wanted to turn Sabarimala into Kerala's Ayodhya agitation. Uttar Pradesh Chief Minister Yogi Adityanath said 'there were many attempts to insult believers' at both holy places and asked them to start an Ayodhya-type agitation at Kerala's hill temple 'to keep their faith'.[24]

The IUML and the Kerala Congress (M), parties that have emerged out of Kerala's Muslim and Christian communities, respectively, also endorsed the agitation. That these parties, the majority of whose supporters are not Hindus, would endorse the agitation against the court verdict is hardly surprising. It was not just because of their political opposition to the ruling LDF government. Rehana Fathima, who attempted to enter Sabarimala, raised the hackles of Muslim organizations. Kerala Muslim Jamaath Council president A. Pookunju said that Rehana Fathima and her family had been 'expelled' from membership of Mahallu – namely from the Muslim community.[25] The Council told the Ernakulam Central Muslim Jamaath to expel her and her family from its membership. This form of social ostracism revealed how conservative sections and religious orthodoxy share the same mindset when it comes to women's rights. The IUML – a part of the UDF – extended its support to the Sabarimala protests. The Muslim League, therefore, also provided legitimacy to the agenda of

[23] *The Week*, 5 November 2018.

[24] *Hindustan Times*, 15 February 2019.

[25] *The Hindu*, 20 October 2018.

the Hindu Right, who they claim are their adversary. On 10 October 2018, the Muslim League held a rally in Changanassey (Kottayam district) to express its solidarity with the protests. The League's general secretary, P.K. Kunhalikutty, who was also a member of parliament from Malappuram, said, 'It is Ayyappa devotees who have to take a decision regarding Sabarimala. Courts should take into consideration the people's mood. Tomorrow, similar kind of judgments may come out regarding the belief system of any other religion.'[26] It is this 'fear' of the judicial reversal of archaic religious customs in the name of enlightenment and emancipation that led the League to express its solidarity with the protests. The Kerala Congress (M) also shared the same thinking, and it drove them to back the Sabarimala protests. This party has its base among the Christian community of central Travancore. Its chairperson at the time, K.M. Mani, said of the Sabarimala issue, 'The state government has cheated all believers in the state, and it can't be allowed to violate age-old customs in the name of gender equality.'[27]

Even as the All-India Congress Committee gingerly welcomed the verdict of the Supreme Court, the Kerala unit went in the other direction. The Indian National Congress's Ramesh Chennithala went on a hunger strike against the verdict. 'The Congress,' he said, 'will take up the agitation for the protection of the ongoing practices of Sabarimala temple in the wake of the Supreme Court order allowing women of all ages into the shrine. The Congress will continue the agitation till the ongoing practices of [the] lord Ayyappa temple are

[26] *Asianet News*, 7 October 2018.

[27] *Samayam Malayalam*, 9 October 2018.

restored'.[28] The UDF essentially validated the Sabarimala agitation, led by the Sangh Parivar forces.

Against this agitation rose a progressive-left dynamic supporting women's entry. It was led by the Left but also sections of Kerala's society that had been marked by Renaissance history. The Women's Wall was the culmination of this dynamic against the reproduction of gender inequality and indignity.

Spontaneous mobilizations of progressive people across the state led to the decision to create a Vanitha Mathil – a women's wall – in Kerala. In late November, the LDF government, at a meeting chaired by Chief Minister Pinarayi Vijayan, decided to give its full support to the creation of a wall of women from Kasaragod to Thiruvananthapuram on 1 January 2019. Representatives from 170 organizations came to a meeting with the government where this decision was taken.[29] The chief minister said that the wall would 'protect the values of [the] Kerala reformation movement and . . . support the state government's stance on the Supreme Court verdict allowing women of all ages to enter the Sabarimala temple'. Furthermore, on New Year's Day, this wall would not permit Kerala to be 'turned into a lunatic asylum'.[30]

Representatives of the majority of the community groups participated in the meeting and adopted a mandate to defend the Renaissance tradition. They formed an organizing committee that comprised SNDP Yogam General Secretary Vellappally Natesan as chairman, KPMS General Secretary

[28] *The New Indian Express*, 4 October 2018.

[29] *The New Indian Express*, 2 December 2018.

[30] *The Hindu*, 1 December 2018.

Punnala Sreekumar as convener and K. Somaprasad as treasurer. The agitators and even leaders of the opposition took an open stand against the decision to create the Women's Wall. Congress leader Ramesh Chennithala said that the wall 'is nothing but poison with a sugar coating as it will lead to communal polarization. The LDF is trying to create a wedge in society through such actions, which will result in polarization along communal and casteist lines'. 'The women's wall is a communal wall which will destroy the communal harmony prevailing in the state,' he said, adding that 'the wall is a challenge to the secular credentials that the state has been upholding all these years. It is going to divide people in the state on communal lines'. [31] This was a remarkable comment – it turned secular into communal and communal into secular.

The campaign for the Women's Wall excited many people across the state. The Sabarimala Karma Samithi organized the Ayyappa Jyothi campaign as a counter-move. There were attempts to sow fear amongst those who would participate in the *Vanitha Mathil*. Kaumudi reported that when the Women's Wall was being formed on New Year's Day, some BJP and RSS workers attacked the Wall at Chettukundu – twenty kilometres south of Kasaragod. When women arrived to line up, they would not let them get in formation. The police lathi-charged these workers, who hurled stones at the women and the police.[32] Social media was flooded with sexist language, designed to create confusion and fear around the Wall.

Despite these challenges, the women of Kerala etched their names in history on New Year's Day, 2019. Over 3.5 to 5 million

[31] *The New Indian Express*, 3 December 2018.

[32] *Kaumudi Online*, 1 January 2019.

built a wall that ran over 620 kilometres from Kasaragod – in the north – to Thiruvananthapuram – in the south. Kerala Health Minister K.K. Shailaja stood at the head of the Wall at Kasaragod and CPI (M) leader Brinda Karat stood at the end of the Wall in the state's capital. They stood for gender justice and Renaissance values. More than a third of the women in Kerala participated in the Wall. These women came from all communities and backgrounds – politicians, workers, peasants and agricultural labourers, homemakers, artists, writers, social activists, bureaucrats, teachers, and journalists. The Women's Wall witnessed the participation of the masses. Kudumbashree activists, Mahatma Gandhi National Rural Employment Guarantee scheme workers, and Asha-Anganwadi workers were the backbone of the women's gathering. According to the Universal Record Forum, this was the longest women's wall ever recorded in the world.[33] 'It is not an exaggeration to say that this was one of the largest mobilizations of women in the world for women's rights. It is certainly larger than the historic women's march in Washington, DC in 2017'.[34]

At 4 p.m., the women stood for fifteen minutes and took a pledge to defend their rights, gender equality, and secularism: '[W]e are taking the pledge that we will stand for equality for women; we resist the attempts to make Kerala a lunatic asylum; and we will fight for secularism'.[35]

At a meeting related to the Wall, Brinda Karat described its significance:

[33] *The Economic Times*, 2 January 2019.

[34] Vijay Prashad, '5.5 Million Women Build Their Wall', *CounterPunch*, 14 January 2019.

[35] *The News Minute*, 1 January 2019.

> The wall had sent a strong message not just to the women of Kerala, but to women all over India. We appeal to the believer women of Kerala to not become pawns in the hands of the RSS, who are using them for a toxic, divisive, and anti-women political goal. It is for you and your girl child that this wall is being built.[36]

The day after the Wall, two women – Bindu Ammini and Kanakadurga – entered the Sabarimala temple.

In Kerala, a thick line was drawn between the Left and the Right on the issue of Sabarimala. The agitation against women's entry turned to severe protests, often descending into violence and leading to continuous hartals. The UDF observed black day and participated in the protests. Meanwhile, the government withstood the agitation, and prevented the state from descending into wholesale chaos. From the day of the Supreme Court verdict itself, the government was prepared to honour the decision and defend it with the full machinery of the state government.

DEFENDING 'CUSTOM' THROUGH VIGILANTISM

The essence of the protests against the Supreme Court verdict on Sabarimala is that they are guided by a patriarchal view. Many women who expressed a desire to go to Sabarimala, and the women who dared to go, were threatened with, or actually faced, physical violence in public. This has alarmed all those who value democracy. In October 2018, after the

[36] *The Hindu*, 2 January 2019.

Supreme Court verdict was delivered on 28 September, when the Sabarimala temple opened for its monthly poojas, protests were organized by a newly emerged group, the Sabarimala Karma Samithi. They set up camps at Nilakkal and Pamba (or Pampa) to stop women between the ages of 10 and 50 who appeared to be going to the temple. Vigilantes flooded into these camps, frazzled and aggressive. They did not distinguish between women who were devotees and women who were journalists. Both were prevented from entering the temple, with women from national television news channels facing harsh treatment and even attack.[37] These vigilantes conducted 'vehicle checks' to ensure that there were no women inside the cars. The BBC reported, 'It was an intimidating atmosphere for journalists – one can only imagine what it was like for any woman wanting to attend the temple.'[38]

In January 2019, Shajila Ali Fathima, a cameraperson for Kairali TV, was assaulted as she filmed the Sabarimala protests in Thiruvananthapuram. There is an image of her with her camera, tears streaming down her face, that came to be widely shared. She recounted the moment with great vividness:

> Like the other camerapersons, I was busy filming BJP workers ripping (possibly CPI(M)) banners when they turned on us. I could hear several voices screaming at me, that I would be killed if the footage I had captured went on air. But I continued to film what was happening in front of me. Then several men began attacking every cameraperson around. It is as if they had pre-planned the

[37] *The Hindu*, 17 October 2018.

[38] BBC, 17 October 2018.

attack on journalists since there were six to eight men around each one of us. When someone tried to snatch my camera, I held on with all my strength, but in the process, I sprained my neck. That was when emotion overtook my resolve. I restarted the camera with some difficulty and began shooting again. By then I was crying. I did feel a bit ashamed that I was crying while on duty. But somehow, I couldn't control . . . my tears.[39]

The media was very upset by this assault. The Kerala Union of Working Journalists boycotted the press conference by BJP chief P.S. Sreedharan Pillai. The Kottayam press club would not allow its hall to be used by K.P. Sasikala, the chief of the Hindu Aikya Vedi. In Kozhikode, the media boycotted the press conference of BJP leader Kummanam Rajasekharan.

Some intellectuals who dared to back the Supreme Court verdict were either threatened or attacked. Writer Sunil P. Ilayidom and Dalit activist Sunny M. Kapikad were threatened when they advocated for women's entry into Sabarimala. National Award-winning filmmaker Priyanandanan was slapped by vigilante men, who poured cow dung over him for his statements on behalf of women's entry into Sabarimala. Unidentified men attacked the ashram of Swami Sandeepananda Giri, a sanyasi who is a firm advocate of women's entry into Sabarimala. 'Last week there was a protest march towards [the] Ashram. Now they have set ablaze the vehicles and left a wreath. They say this is just a warning. I will continue to fight against such attacks.'[40]

[39] *The Telegraph*, 4 January 2019.

[40] *India Today*, 'Right-wing goons attacked my ashram for supporting

A series of hartals by the right-wing forces were called by the Sabarimala Karma Samithi. According to the police and media reports, hundreds of government-owned buses and other public property were damaged in the Sabarimala hartals. The damage amounted to crores of rupees. Reports of attacks on several offices of the Communist Party of India (Marxist), the Communist Party of India, and the houses of their leaders emerged. RSS sent their cadre into the Sabarimala temple complex. Inside the complex, Valsan Thillankeri, senior RSS leader from Kannur, coordinated the protests.

When the BJP state president said that the present developments around Sabarimala were a 'golden opportunity', its meaning was more political than religious. Subsequent political statements by the senior leaders of the party made this clear. BJP national president Amit Shah told a public meeting in Kannur, 'The BJP will take over the protest of the Ayyappa devotees. We will not mind throwing out the government if the Kerala government tries to steamroll the traditions of the Sabarimala temple'.[41] BJP state chief P.S. Sreedharan Pillai was as blatant:

> The protest is not against the issue of entry of women into the temple but against the communist government in the state. Communists are trying to destroy the temple; our protest is against the communists.[42]

The UDF, the opposition coalition in Kerala, was not far

Sabarimala verdict: Swami Sandeepanada Giri', 27 October 2018.

41 *Outlook*, 27 October 2018.

42 *India Today*, 19 November 2018.

behind and stood with the Sabarimala protests. In the days just after the Supreme Court verdict, Congress leader Ramesh Chennithala said that the state was 'cheating Hindus'. The Congress, he said, offered its support 'to those whose sentiments have been hurt by the verdict'. He said that the Congress was for 'retaining the customs and practices of all religions'.[43] The question of the Constitution was set aside. Chennithala went on a day-long fast to 'save the custom and tradition of the Sabarimala temple'. 'This fast,' he said, 'is just the beginning of our agitation. Congress will support Ayyappa devotees to protect the custom'. He was not alone among the Congress leadership. Mullapally Ramachandran, then president of the Congress party in Kerala, said, 'The Congress's consistent stand is that women belonging to the restricted age bracket shouldn't be allowed entry into Sannidhanam'.[44] Based on this position, the Congress party launched five *padayathras* across Kerala in November 2018. These padayathras were led by senior Congress leaders, including Members of the Legislative Assembly (MLAs). During this agitation, K. Sudhakaran, one of these leaders, said, 'Women of menstruation age [sic] will be blocked if they attempt to enter [the] Sabarimala shrine'.[45] The Congress and its UDF allies organized protests at Nilakkal against the imposition of Section 144 of the Indian Penal Code – the promulgation of which bans rioting. When two women finally entered the temple in January, the Congress Party observed a 'black day' in protest.

[43] *Scroll*, 7 October 2018.

[44] *The New Indian Express*, 16 November 2018.

[45] *The New Indian Express*, 14 November 2018.

Braving the Muscle

Madhavi (age 40), from Andhra Pradesh, was the first person who tried to climb the Sabarimala hills toward the temple. On 17 October 2018, Madhavi and her parents were accompanied by the police beyond the hill shrine at Pamba. Director General of Kerala State Police Lokanath Behera said that anyone who tried to block the devotees would be arrested. Ten minutes into the trek, everything fell apart. The vigilantes shouted at her and her family, trying to intimidate them as they walked up the hill. As NDTV reported, 'Protesters were relentless as they chased Madhavi and her family shouting slogans'.[46] The police said that they would stay close to her, but the violent atmosphere was too much for Madhavi and her parents. They turned back.

The next day, Suhasini Raj of *The New York Times* and a foreign colleague tried to make the trek to Sabarimala, but they, too, faced the intimidating vigilante men. Raj tried to say that she had come to do her work, not to pray, but this was not sufficient for the men. Despite police protection, Raj and her colleague felt very unsafe. As she put it, 'I had reached halfway, and then the protests grew stronger. I was hit by a stone and then we decided to return. The police had provided us all the security'.[47]

The violence began to spread beyond the pathways leading to the Sabarimala temple complex. The Kochi home of Rehana Fathima, who tried to enter Sabarimala on 19 October, was ransacked by vigilantes. Bindu Thankam Kalyani, a teacher

[46] NDTV, 17 October 2018.

[47] NDTV, 18 October 2018.

and Dalit activist, tried to enter Sabarimala on 22 October. She received death threats at her home in Kozhikode, from where she was eventually evicted.

Even the declaration to go to Sabarimala was enough for provocation. The social media attack on Bindu Thankam Kalyani had begun as soon as she made public her intention to go to Sabarimala. *Mathrubhumi* reported, 'In a controversial move, a woman was dismissed from service for observing fast to visit Sabarimala temple. The woman was working at the sales department of a private institution in Kozhikode.'[48]

In the noisy atmosphere created by the calls to 'fight to protect faith', basic questions of women's right to dignity and equality were surrendered. Crude and insensitive jokes, verbal abuse, threats of all kinds, and obscene social media campaigns filled the air. Malayalam movie actor Kollam Thulasi said shockingly, 'You mothers should go to Sabarimala. Because some women will go there. They should be torn into two pieces. One portion should be thrown into [the streets of] Delhi and another into the room of the Chief Minister.'[49] Union minister Smriti Irani offered a relatively incoherent comment:

> I believe I have a right to pray, but I don't have the right to desecrate. That is the difference we need to recognise and respect. So, the difference is, I am nobody to speak on the Supreme Court verdict because I am currently [a] serving cabinet minister. But just plain common sense . . .. Would you take sanitary napkins, steeped in menstrual blood, and walk into a friend's home? You would not. And would

[48] *Mathrubhumi* English Edition, 17 October 2018.

[49] *The Indian Express*, 13 October 2018.

you think it is respectful to do the same when you walk into the house of God? That is the difference.[50]

Congress leader and former president of the TDB, Prayar Gopalakrishnan said, outrageously, that 'letting women inside the shrine will lead to immoral activities. We don't want to convert it into a sex tourism spot like Thailand'. He later repeated himself that Sabarimala is 'not a place for sex tourism'.[51] K. Sudhakaran, at present the president of the Kerala Pradesh Congress Committee, made a bizarre statement: 'Menstruation is impurity. No government or Court has the right to change people's beliefs and faith. Instead, it is their responsibility to protect religious beliefs. The custom precedes [the] Constitution'.[52]

In late October, Balamma (age 47) climbed unnoticed towards the temple complex. She had no police protection. Vigilante men surrounded her and asked her for her identity card. Balamma had a panic attack and had to be escorted out by an ambulance.[53] Kavitha and Rehana got to within one hundred metres of the entrance of the shrine. Vasanthi and Aadhiseshi were only able to get within about two hundred metres from Sabarimala. All of them faced the vigilante mob, which appeared to be guided by the RSS men who had taken up a vigil inside the Sabarimala complex.

On 6 November, Lalitha Ravi (from Thrissur) was blocked as she entered the temple. 'A crowd surrounded the woman'

[50] *The Telegraph*, 23 October 2018.

[51] *The Asian Age*, 19 October 2018.

[52] *Mathrubhumi*, 3 October 2018.

[53] Times Now News, 21 October 2018.

and 'In the mild scuffle there, Lalitha's foot was injured'. She was 52, outside the ten to fifty age group, but that did not matter. She showed the men her Aadhaar card, but they pushed it aside. Lalitha had gone to the temple to make offerings for her newborn grandson. None of this mattered. The police had to register a case against 200 people 'for rioting, unlawful assembly, protest against the Supreme Court verdict, and attempted murder and assault on a woman with intent to outrage her modesty.[54] It seemed like any woman was to be barred from entry into Sabarimala by the vigilantes.

Finally, on 2 January 2019, two women – Kanakadurga and Bindu Ammini – entered the temple. Kanakadurga faced harsh treatment from her family. She alleged that her mother-in-law beat her, and that she was evicted from her home. Both received threats of a credible and dangerous sort. On 18 January, the Supreme Court said both should receive police protection.

The extent of the authority and powers of the chief priest of Sabarimala also became subjects for public discussion. The priest, Kandararu Rajeevaru, said that if women enter the temple, 'We have decided to lock the temple and hand over the keys and leave. I stand with the devotees'.[55] Then, when news came of Kanakadurga and Bindu's entry into Sabarimala, Kandararu Rajeevaru closed the temple, apparently to conduct purification rituals. This decision, which arose out of considering their presence as impure, was not only against the essence of the Supreme Court verdict but also against the stand of the TDB, which owns the temple. Board president A.

[54] *The Times of India*, 7 November 2018.

[55] NDTV, 19 October 2018.

Padmakumar said, 'We have decided to seek explanation from the Thanthri about the circumstances that led him to perform the rituals. His act was against the Supreme Court order'.[56]

The most violent protests took place after the successful entry of Kanakadurga and Bindu into Sabarimala. The Sabarimala Karma Samithi called for a hartal on 3 January. Roads were blocked, police stations attacked, and police personnel injured. Over a hundred Kerala State Road Transport Corporation buses were damaged. Praveen, an RSS district leader in Thiruvananthapuram, was arrested in connection with throwing bombs at the Nedumangad police station. The Kerala police arrested 745 people and took another 628 into preventive custody.[57]

Never Mind the Local Community!

Meanwhile, reactions from the Adivasi community that used to live in the forest region around Sabarimala also emerged in the debate about the claims over Sabarimala. The Mala Araya community had been alleging for long time that they were forcibly removed from the Sabari hills, their rights to Sabarimala taken from them – including their practice of lighting the *Makaravilakku*. 'I have done enough research to prove that the temple once belonged to our community and was taken away by the Pandalam palace after driving out our forefathers from the vicinity', said P.K. Sajeev, founder and general secretary of the Aikya Mala Araya Maha Sabha. According to Sajeev's research, Sabarimala temple's presiding

[56] *The Economic Times*, 4 January 2019.

[57] *The Indian Express*, 3 January 2019.

deity – Lord Ayyappa – was thought to have been born to a Mala Araya couple, Kandan and Karuthamma, in a cave in Ponnambalamedu near Sabarimala. Araya priests used to conduct the *thenabhishekam* – the bathing of the idol with honey.'Our forefathers performed this ritual at Sabarimala until 1950', Sajeev said. 'I know the descendants of the Mala Araya family that lit the Makara Vilakku (lamp) for generation,' he added. 'We want to conduct our traditional rituals at Sabarimala and light the Makara Vilakku.'[58]

Historians agree that the temple was more or less rooted in the local community, with the Mala Arayas in charge of the rituals before 1950. 'Hardly anybody went there', said historian M.G.S. Narayanan. '[I]t had no all-Kerala importance until it was rebuilt following a 1950 fire.'[59] Rajan Gurukkal, also a historian, concurs:

> An insignificant shrine deep inside the forest, and hence outside the Brahmanical tradition, the Ayyappa temple used to be visited in the olden days by people belonging to various tribes such as Malapantaram, Ulatar, Mannan, Narikkuravar, and a few low-caste people settled along the fringes, besides a pilgrimage from Tamil Nadu, annually during the Makara Sankrama. This tradition continued until recent times, accounting for the present claim of tribal heritage of the temple.[60]

The Adivasi communities are in a legal battle to establish

[58] *The Telegraph*, 7 November 2018.

[59] Rohan Manoj, 'Sabarimala: Restrictions On Women A "Recent Phenomenon"', *Outlook*, 22 October 2018.

[60] Rajan Gurukkal, 'Manufactured legends', *Frontline*, 1 February 2019.

their right over the temple. The legal battle over the question of women's entry, too, is far from settled. As this book goes to press, the Supreme Court has referred, having kept a final judgment on the review petitions pending, the case for a larger bench to hear.

PART 2

HOW SABARIMALA BECAME SABARIMALA

ROOTS OF THE TEMPLE, HINDU TRADITION AND LEGENDS

In the old days, faith and religion had its own tempo, rooted so deeply as it was in the natural world. In Kerala, various castes and Adivasis consecrated parts of forests and groves into sacred places (generally called *kavus*), which they dedicated to their own divine beings. The common deities in these *kavus*, mostly very local figures, are Bhagavathi, Nagam, Amman, Ayyappan, etc. The *kavus* had names such as Sarppakavu, Ayyappankavu, Theyyakavu, Mundyankavu, Hanumankavu, Bhagavathikavu, and Ammankavu. Rituals in these sacred groves were conducted by the respective communities of the area.

The premodern history of Sabarimala and the Ayyappa deity is tough terrain for exploration, but it is likely to have its roots in the traditions of the local cults in sacred groves. 'Before the 1950s, the Sabarimala temple was part of the local traditions of its area. It became known only after a 1950 arson incident', according to historian M.G.S. Narayanan. Much like other village temples, it was a place of worship mainly for the local population.[1] The ancient and medieval references to Sabarimala are not available. But we have references about the temple from the late medieval period. The Pandalam Adamanam (mortgage by the Pandalam ruling family) in Malayalm year 969 (1793) mentions that the royal family is mortgaging the revenue returns, including that of the Sabarimala temple to the Travancore state.[2] References to the

[1] *Deccan Chronicle*, 10 October 2018.

[2] Pandalam adamanam, Malayalam year 969, in T.K. Velupillai, Travancore

rights of the descendants of Vavar, conferred by the Pandalam ruler in Malayalam year 968 (1792) in Sabarimala of the same century are available.[3] However, Ward and Conner's text on Travancore published in 1863 (survey conducted in 1816-20) is one of the earliest available references that gives details and descriptions of Sabarimala and its surroundings.[4] William Henry Horsley's Memoir of Travancore, Historical and Statistical, published in 1839, is another earlier text describing Sabarimala. There are also myriad legends and stories about Lord Ayyappa, including his birth as *Hariharaputhra*, the child born to the god Siva and Mohini (one of the avatars of Vishnu), the adoption of Manikanta by the Pandalam Raja, the heroic efforts of a young Ayyappa to defeat a wild leopard, his battle with a local warrior named Vavar, and his path of celibacy. These are legends, collected by local chroniclers.

Behind these legends and these tales lies a much more conventional history for Sabarimala – it was a site imbued with heterogeneous influence that would only in the twentieth century be fully absorbed into a homogenous Hindu tradition. Radhika Sekar, a religious studies scholar, shows us that the myths and legends of Ayyappa are not found in any of the major Puranic texts. 'The only Sanskrit text that narrates the story of Ayyappa in any detail', Sekar points out in her 1992 monograph, 'is the 19th-century text *Bhutanathopakhyanam* . . . considered the primary text of the cultus.'[5] Unlike the

[3] Speech by Dr T.S. Syamkumar, 6 November 2018. Available here: https://www.youtube. com/watch?v=gulsMc2HI2k&t=916s

[4] Lt Benjamin Swain Ward and Lt. Peter Eyre Conner, *Memoir of the Survey of Travancore and Cochin States*, vol. 1, 1863, p. 136.

[5] Radhika Sekar, *The Śabarimalai Pilgrimage and Ayyappan Cultus*, Delhi: Motilal Banarsidass Publishers, 1992, p. 15.

Puranic cults, the Ayyappa cult is traditionally not found in northern India; instead, it is confined to Kerala, Karnataka, and Tamil Nadu. Eminent Indian sociologist M.N. Srinivas argues that Ayyappa is a South Indian deity. He says that 'it is interesting to note that the cult of Ayyappa or Sastha doesn't occur in the Kannada, Telugu, and Maharashtra countries. It seems to be confined to Coorg, the west coast south of Mangalore and the Tamil country, especially to the southern and western part of it'.[6] In Kerala, the earliest reference to the god Ayyappan is in the tenth-eleventh century Thiruvalla copper plates. There is also a coinage of the term 'Ayyappan Emberuman'.[7] In Malayalam year 665, we find a reference to 'Ayyan Chatha'.[8] There is also the coinage of the term 'Ayyappan Chathavu' in ancient records of Travancore.[9] Ayyappa cults are found among the Kodavas (Coorgs) of Karnataka and across Kerala.[10]

One of the most popularized legends regarding Ayyappa is that this deity is the same as Dharmasastha, mentioned in the *Skanda Purana*. Does this mean that Ayyappa should be seen, historically, as part of the Hindu puranic traditions? Scholars such as T.A. Gopinatha Rao argue that 'Sastha should

[6] M.N. Srinivas, 'A Brief Note on Ayyappa, the South Indian Deity' in K.M. Kapadia (ed.), *Professor Ghurye Felicitation Volume*, Popular Book Depot, 1954, p. 243.

[7] T. Gopinatha Rao, *Travancore Archeological Series*, Vol. 2, Part 3, Madras, Methodist publishing house, 1910-13, p. 149.

[8] T.K. Velupillai, *Travancore State Manual*, Vol. 2, Govt. of Travancore, 1940, Appendix, p.19.

[9] Rajaraja Varma Raja, *Kerala Society papers, Some Travancore Dynastic Records (A.D. 544-1677)*, First Series, p.19.

[10] M.N. Srinivas, *Religion and Society Among the Coorgs of South India*, Bombay: Asia Publishing House, 1952, pp. 225-26.

have been a very common name and the deity was perhaps once better known by that name in the Tamil country; this is deducible from the fact that in all examples of grammars of declension, inflexion, etc., the subject of a sentence is Sattan (Sastha) just as the Sanskrit grammarians usually employ the name of Devadatta'. He further says that 'this deity who is very peculiar to the Dravida country does not appear to have been known to the region north of the Godavari. In no early Sanskrit work is the deity mentioned. Even the dictionaries do not record this name and give its origin'.[11] Sastha is also given the name Hariharaputhra. In the *Vishnupurana* we hear that Vishnu, seeing the quarrel between Devas and Asuras over the distribution of *Amrit*, assumed the form of a charming damsel. Texts such as the *Sri Bhagavatam*, *Amsumadagama,* and *Suprabhedagama* tell the story of how Hara or Siva fell in love with Hari or Vishnu – in the form of Mohini, and their union produced Hariharaputhra. However, Gopinatha Rao believed that this 'puranic story [was] invented for his origin at a latter period of the history of Hindu iconography'. Rao's conclusion was that 'Buddha as conceived and worshiped in the Tamil country was ultimately included in the Hindu pantheon'.[12] V. Narayana Pillai, in his presentation at the Indian History Congress in 1939, disagreed with Rao and said that 'Sastha is not the Hinduized Buddha'. He reaches the conclusion that 'the Hinduism of Kerala, as with the rest of India, was the result of a fusion of Aryan and non-Aryan cults. The Sastha worship, which is still prevalent among all classes of the

[11] T.A. Gopinatha Rao, *Elements of Hindu Iconography*, Volume 2, Part 2, Madras: The Law Printing House, 1916, p. 486.

[12] Ibid., p. 488.

people, primitive as well as civilized, is a Dravidian element, which was absorbed by the Aryans in the course of the racial and cultural fusion that went on in the country'.[13]

There is also a claim made that the Sastha cult emerges out of the Yaksha cult. Because Ayyappa wears a bell around his neck and is called Manikanta, some say that he is like Ghantika Yaksha. But Ghantika Yaksha has a bull-head, while Ayyappa does not.[14] Furthermore, 'whenever the deity has been installed with consort (Sree Prabha) and son (Sree Sathyaka) or with two consorts (Sree Poorna and Sree Pushkala), the temple with this deity falls under the concept of Lord Sastha. Lord Ayyappa is a brahmachaari or baala-yogi having no consorts.[15]

The Buddhist texts show us that Sastha is used as synonymous with Buddha. In the fourth-century text composed by Amarasimha, *Amarakosha*, the name Sastha is used synonymously with Buddha.[16] A verse establishes this connection:

Muneendra: sreeghana:
sastha muni:
sakhya munisthuya:
sasakhya simha:
sarvartha sidha:

[13] V. Narayana Pillai, 'Sasta Cult In Travancore. Is it a relic of Buddhism?' in *Proceedings of the Indian History Congress*, Vol. 3, 1939, p. 236.

[14] Sekar, *The Śabarimalai Pilgrimage and Ayyappan Cultus*, p. 23.

[15] S. Jayashankar, 'Temples of Kannoor District' in *Census of India Special Studies – Kerala*, 1999, p. 33.

[16] Kaikulangara Ramavariar (trans.), *Amarakosham*, Kollam: S.T. Reddiar & Sons, 1950, p. 4.

saudhodanichasa[17]

Old Buddhist texts use the term Sastha to refer to an *acharya* ('one who advises').[18] 'It seems that the Tamils accept all references in ancient literature to *Sastha* as synonymous with *Aiyanar/Aiyappa*, although the texts give absolutely no information about these *Sasthas* apart from the name.'[19]

Hindu temples in the *Ithihasa-Purana* tradition were largely built after the Brahmin migration to Kerala. It was around the eighth-ninth century that migration in significant numbers took place, and Brahmin settlements established. Historians agree that most of these settlements or Brahmin villages were developed in the wetland plains as they were more fertile than hilly regions. Naturally, their temples were also located in these regions. Interestingly, the Sabarimala temple complex is outside the wetland area.

As historian K.N. Ganesh notes, 'In the earlier period god Ayyappa was worshipped most often in Ayyappan *kavus* (sacred groves). A well-built and grand temple structure for Ayyappa was rare in Kerala villages.'[20] This is borne out by V. Narayana Pillai's observation: 'These village temples are unpretentious in their structure. In many cases, they are mere walled enclosures without even a roof, located in Kavus, usually a cluster of trees and creepers.'[21] The records compel

[17] Ibid. (All of the above were names used to refer to the Buddha.)

[18] S.K. Vasanthan, *Nammal Nadanna Vazhikal, Kerala Charithravum Samskaravum* (The Roads We Walked, Kerala's History and Culture), Thrissur: Malayala Padana Gaveshana Kendram, 2011, p. 41.

[19] Ibid., p. 40.

[20] Personal interview with K.N. Ganesh, Kozhikode, 14 October 2016.

[21] V. Narayana Pillai, 'Sasta Cult in Travancore. Is it a Relic of Buddhism?' in

one to reach the understanding that the Ayyappa cult, in its earlier history, was much more aligned to the heterogeneous local cults than to the Puranic tradition.

Traces of Ayyanar and Tribal Claims

One way that many scholars have established this ancestry has been to highlight the connection between the horseman god *Ayyanar* of the land of the Tamils and the lord *Ayyappa* of Sabarimala. Radhika Sekar points out, for instance, 'Ayyanar is basically a village tutelary deity, worshipped by the lower castes. Ayyappa is sometimes associated with the Ayyanar of Tamil Nadu.'[22] Gopinatha Rao finds that they are the same god.[23] In Tamil Nadu, Ayyanar is worshipped as a village guardian god. 'Velar priests (non- Brahmin potters) can be found as priests in Aiyanar temples all over Tamil Nadu.'[24] Kjaerholm writes, '[H]e is an important village god, and his temples are found only in villages, never in towns.'[25]

Writings on Ayyanar (such as *Ayyanarvillupattu*) depict him as a great warrior and, with his lieutenant Karuppuswami, as a protector of villages against floods and evil spirits. The two of them are shown in eternal combat against evil forces. Ayyanar is known as a horse rider, a warrior god. Near shrines

Proceedings of the Indian History Congress, Vol. 3, 1939, p. 236.

22 Sekar, *The Śabarimalai Pilgrimage and Ayyappan Cultus*, p. 19.

23 Gopinatha Rao, *Elements of Hindu Iconography*, p. 487.

24 Lars, Kjaerholm, 'Myth, Pilgrimage and Fascination in the Aiyappa Cult. A View From Field Work in Tamil Nadu', *South Asia Research*, Vol. 2, Nov. 1982, p. 32.

25 Ibid., p. 25.

to Ayyanar, there are often temples to Karuppuswami.[26] In front of Ayyanar temples, there are often statues of Ayyanar and Karuppuswami on horseback.[27] In Kottavasal – on the way to Achankovil in the Sabarimala hill region – there is a temple for Karuppuswami. Inside the Sabarimala temple complex itself, there is a Karuppuswami installation near the pathinettampadi. The presence of Karuppuswami near Ayyappa indicates the closeness of the Ayyanar cult to the Sabarimala Ayyappa cult. The story of Ayyappa's fight with a tiger offers a mirror to the many stories of Ayyanar as a warrior god.

An unfortunate methodological limitation of our historical studies is that it is mainly built around available documents and records. Though oral history and other new trends help to match the lacuna, history is still written around dominant records. The tribal claims over Sabarimala testify to this lacuna. The descendants of Mala Araya tribes, who used to live in the hills around Sabarimala, claimed for years that the historical ownership of Sabarimala rested with them and god Ayyappa was a member of their family. They also claimed that even the priestly duties were performed by their forefathers. These are oral accounts. We have some texts pointing towards the tribal relationship with Sabarimala. Samual Mateer, a British Missionary, in his book *Native Life in Travancore*, quotes Rev. W.J. Richards to describe the Mala Araya relation with Sabarimala:

[26] Lars Kjaerholm, 'Aiyanar and Aiyappan Cult in Tamil Nadu: Change and Continuity in South Indian Hinduism', *Folk: Dansk etnografisk Tidsskrift*, vol. 26, 1984, pp. 67–92.

[27] Ibid.

Talanani was a priest or oracle-revealer of the hunting deity, Ayappan, whose chief shrine is in Savarimala, a hill among the Travancore Ghats. The duty of Talanani was to deck himself out, as already described in this book, in his sword, bangles, beads, &c., and highly frenzied with excitement and strong drink, dance in a convulsive horrid fashion before his idols, and reveal in unearthly shrieks what the god had decreed on any particular matter. He belonged to the Hill Arayan village of Eruma-para (the rock of the she-buffalo), some eight or nine from Melkavu, and was most devoted to his idolatry, and rather remarkable in his peculiar way of showing his zeal. When the pilgrims from his village used to go to Sabarimala – a pilgrimage, which is always, for fear of the tigers and other wild beasts, performed in companies of forty or fifty – our hero would give out that he was not going, and yet when they reached the shrine of their devotions, there before them was the sorcerer, so that he was both famous among his fellows and favoured of the gods.

Now, while things were in this way, Talanani was killed by the neighbouring Chogans during one of his drunken bouts, and the murderers, burying his body in the depths of the jungle, thought that their crime would never be found out; but the tigers, Ayappan's dogs, in respect to so true a friend of their master, scratched open the grave, and, removing the corpse, laid it on the ground. The wild elephants found the body, and reverently took it where friends might discover it, and a plague of small pox having attacked the Chogans, another oracle declared it was sent by Sastavu (the Travancore hill boundary god, also called Chattan or Sattan) in anger at the crime that had been committed; and that the evil would not abate until the murderers made an image of the dead priest and worshipped it . . . . All the descendants of Talanani are Christians, the results of the Rev. Henry Baker's work. The last heir who was in possession of the idol, sword, bangle, beads, and wand of the sorcerer, handed them over to the Rev. W. J. Richards in 1881, when he had charge for a time of Melkavu.[28]

L.A. Krishna Iyer, ethnographer of Travancore princely state, who did extensive studies on Travancore tribes, made meticulous observation of the social life of Mala Arayas.

'Being afraid of attacks by wild elephants, he (Malayarayan) takes shelter in it (tree house) with his family at night and drives off wild elephants by shouting "Ayyappa" writes Iyer.[29] It shows that Ayyappa was their familiar, protective god.

The Sabarimala Ayyappa worship was not confined to this tribe only. According to Krishna Iyer, the Ullatans tribe fondly worship Ayyappa and 'worship Sastha at Sabarimala, which is said to have been in the joint possession of Pandalam Raja, Kakkattu Potti, the Perinadu folk, and the Kochuvelan (headman of the tribe). The association of the Ullatans with Sastha is one of hoary antiquity'.[30]

[28] Samuel Mateer, *Native life in Travancore*, W.H. Allen & Co., London, 1883, pp. 75-77.

[29] L.A. Krishna Iyer, *Travancore Tribes and Castes*, Vol 1, Govt. Press, Trivandrum, 1937, pp. 168-69.

[30] L.A. Krishna Iyer, *Travancore Tribes and Castes*, Vol 1, Govt. Press, Trivandrum, 1939, pp. 212-13.

Traces of Buddhism?

'While the whole of South India was, for a long time, under the spell of the Buddha and Jaina religious faiths, Travancore, itself a portion of Dravida, was equally, if not more so, under their influence. The Buddha faith was firmly established in the very centre of Malabar, in a place called Srimulavasam. The large number of Buddha images found in the Mavelikkara, Kunnattur, Karunagapalli, and Ambalapuzha taluks, represent at least as many temples of Buddha in as many places' writes Gopinatha Rao, the Archaeological superintendent of Travancore state who had discovered many important inscriptions. He also says that 'in Southern India, Buddhism flourished till about the end, at least, of the 13th century A.D'.[31]

The Western Ghats, the mountains that line the western edge of India, once had a significant Buddhist presence. The existence of Buddhism in Kerala can be traced also from the report of Chinese pilgrim Xuanzang (602-664 CE). After visiting Ta-lo-pi-ch'a (Dravida) region, he moved to the south, coming to Mo-lo-Kiu-ch'a (Malakuta). He says that 'almost all the Buddhist temples in Malakuta were in ruins'.[32] This means that there was Buddhist presence even before his visit in Malakuta. He also describes the Mo-la-ye (Malaya) mountains. 'Malakuta mentioned by him is considered by scholars as synonymous with Malinadu or the west coast of

[31] T.A. Gopinatha Rao, *Travancore Archeological Series*, Vol. 2, Part 2 (Bauddha and Jaina Vestiges in Travancore), Madras, Methodist publishing house, 1910-13, pp. 115-16.

[32] Hikosaka Shu, 'Buddhism in Tamil Nadu: A New Perspective', Institute of Asian Studies, Chennai, 1989, p. 84.

Kerala extending from Kanyakumari in [the] south to Periyar River in the north.'[33]

The Tamil text *Thiruvilaiyadal* ('The Divine Game') says that there were eight prominent monasteries and eight thousand monks in the Ghats in the early eighth century.[34] Some argue that the Mo-la-ye mountain bordering the sea may either represent the Malabar Ghats generally, or, more probably, the detached mass of the Ghats south of the Coimbatore gap.

Some argue that the area around the Sabarimala temple had a strong Buddhist influence. The forest around the temple complex is commonly or symbolically called the Poonkavanam. 'It is said that the Buddhists and Jains used to name their places of worship using words that resonate with flowers (*pookal*).'[35] Buddhist monasteries had neem trees in front of them as a symbol of knowledge. 'The Ayyappan *kovils* ("God's residence", or temples) have neem trees in front of them as well.'[36] S.K. Vasanthan finds that 'Ambalappuzha and Alangad – associated with the Sabarimala pilgrimage – are also places with a history of Buddhist influence. Both these places have much importance in *Petta Thullal*, a significant ritual associated with the Sabarimala pilgrimage.'[37]

[33] Ajit Kumar, 'Buddhism in Kerala and its Socio-cultural Ramification', *History Today*, No. 19, 2018, p. 179.

[34] Ajay Sekher, 'Pallykanam and Pullykanam: Western Ghats and an Ecocultural Crisis', in Ajaysekher.net, a blog by Ajay Sekher (Last accessed 19 March 2020). Available here: https://ajaysekher.net/2013/06/23/pallykanam-vagaman

[35] Vasanthan, *Kerala Charithravum Samskaravum*, p. 41.

[36] Iyyankode Sreedharan, 'Ayyappanum Krishnanum' [Ayyappa and Krishna], *Yukthi Rekha*, September 1983, p. 15.

[37] Vasanthan, *Kerala Charithravum Samskaravum*, p. 41.

The 1931 Census Report on Travancore makes a bold claim:

> Sastha, the name often given to Buddha in Buddhistic scriptures, was admitted into the Hindu pantheon. The famous Sastha temples now existing in Sabarimala, Thakkala, and other places in Travancore were originally none other than temples dedicated to Buddha. . . . Besides these temples, several remains of Buddhist viharas and chaityas are still seen in different parts of this country.[38]

Contemporary scholarship is not far from this view. M. Sreekala Nair points out that Ayyappa is similar to Avalokiteswara in many respects.[39] Inside the temple is an image of Ayyappa seated, a *panchaloha* image of him, pleasant and youthful.[40] His right arm, with a mudra, rests on the knee of his right leg, while his left arm rests on the left leg, his legs folded in a *yogapeeda*. Some scholars see this image as mimetic of the statues of Buddha as he meditates. 'But many historians including Rajan Gurukkal & P.C. Alaxander refuted this claim'.[41] The Hindu Agamas, such as Amsumadbhedagama, Suprabhedagama, and Karanagama, offer detailed installation procedures of the Sastha idol (it is to be noted that these texts

[38] N. Kunjan Pillai, *Census of India, 1931*, vol. XXVIII: Travancore, Trivandrum: The Superintendent, Govt. Press, 1932, p. 334.

[39] Sreekala M. Nair, 'Facets of Kerala's Religiosity: An Overview', in *Introduction to Kerala Studies*, vol. 1, ed. J.V. Vilanilam, Antony Palackal and Sunny Luke, New Jersey: IISAC, 2012, p. 185.

[40] An alloy of five metals, traditionally made with gold, silver, copper, zinc, and iron.

[41] For more, see P.C. Alexander, *Buddhism in Kerala*, Annamalai University, 1949; Rajan Gurukkal, 'Yes, Sabarimala is in Peril, but Not the Way You Think', *Outlook*, 5 November 2018.

do not offer a uniform description of how the installation should be done). The present Ayyappa idol in Sabarimala was probably installed after the 1950 fire based on these texts. But the question remains if there is no Agama for the installation of Ayyappan, and if Sastha and Ayyappan are the same, then what about the consorts mentioned in these Agama texts?

Sreedhara Menon writes that 'it cannot be denied that Buddhism had exercised its own influence on the development of the Sastha cult in Kerala'. His verdict is worth quoting in full:

> The Sabarimala pilgrims observe strict vows of nonviolence, vegetarianism, and abstinence from worldly pleasures for about two months prior to their pilgrimage and this is considered to be a practice reminiscent of the Buddhist doctrine of Ahimsa. Further, the pilgrims do not observe caste distinctions during the period of their vow and this also accords well with the Buddhist emphasis on castelessness and cosmopolitanism. The sing-song repetition of *Saranamayyappa* by the lakhs of Hindu pilgrims who go to the shrine of the Dharmasastha at Sabarimala also remains one of the triple Saranam formula of the Buddha, the Dharma, and the Sangha of the Buddhists. The locations of the famous Sastha temples of Kerala like those of Sabarimala, Achankovil, and Aryankavu in the interior of the forests is cited as additional support to the Buddhist theory because it is believed that the Buddhists preferred to live in faraway secluded places.[42]

[42] A. Sreedhara Menon, *A Survey of Kerala History*, Kottayam: DC Books, 2007, p. 87.

'The strict vegetarianism and *Saranamantras* sung as a part of the devotional songs to Ayyappa have close resemblance to Buddhist ethical norms and *Saranatrayas*.'[43] Chanting '*saranam*' during the pilgrimage is believed to have resonance with the Buddhist mantra:

Buddham Saranam Gachhaami
Dhammam Saranam Gacchaami
Sangham Saranam Gacchaami

The Sabarimala pilgrimage is a collective pilgrimage. 'The Ayyappan cultus seems to fall under the criteria of a revitalization movement but with some essential differences', writes Radhika Sekar. 'It seems to be a product of collective vision.'[44] This collective vision and this collective journey are related to the Buddhist idea of the *sangham* (group). The Ayyappa sangham, people like S.N. Sadasivan, point out, mimics the Buddhist sangham. The *mandala pooja* in *mandala kalam* at Sabarimala is a unique ritual associated with this temple. Again, many scholars argue that the ritual has links to the concept of the *mandala*, which is rooted in Buddhist tantrism. The month of Pausha (corresponding to Dhanu-Makaram of the Malayalam calendar), when Ashoka, after his conversion to Buddhism, celebrated his coronation and adopted the title of *Devanampriya*, is sacred to Buddhists.[45] It is in this month that the Makaravilakku pilgrimage to

[43] Nair, 'Facets of Kerala's Religiosity', p. 185.

[44] Sekar, *The Śabarimalai Pilgrimage and Ayyappan Cultus*, p. 6.

[45] S.N. Sadasivan, *A Social History of India*, Delhi: APH Publishing, 2000, p. 121.

Sabarimala takes place. According to many, a final Buddhist influence is key: Sabarimala, unlike many of the wetland Brahminical temples, has always allowed people – but, probably later, not all women – into the temple irrespective of caste and even religious differences.

Ayyappan and a Muslim Saint

Dominique-Sila Khan, a scholar of religion, writes of the 'strange anomaly' of Sabarimala Ayyappa temple, where you first visit a Muslim 'saint' named Vavar in a Mosque in Erumeli before proceeding to visit Ayyappa. There are different versions of the legend regarding Ayyappa's relation with Vavar.

One day during a hunting expedition, the ruler of Pandalam found a baby on the bank of the Pamba river. As the king was childless, he decided to adopt the infant and gave the boy the name Manikanda. After a while, a son was born to the king of Pandalam, but he still considered Manikanda his elder son and heir. The jealous Queen feigned illness and, having won the confidence of the court's physicians, made them declare that the only cure for her disease was tigress' milk. Manikanda agreed to undertake this seemingly impossible task and started for the forest. On his way, he met Vavar, whom he defeated in a duel. The Muslim pirate went on to become his friend and faithful lieutenant.[46]

According to another version of the legend, Vavar and his men lived in boats and plundered those who came that way on trade and also those who lived in the coastal regions of the

[46] Dominique-Sila Khan, *Sacred Kerala: A Spiritual Pilgrimage*, New Delhi: Penguin, 2009, pp. 62-63.

Kingdom of Kayamkulam. Since Vavar distributed the major portion of his plundered goods among his followers and the poor people, he had a large number of followers. His activities centred around the ports of Kayamkulam and Karunagapilly. [47]

Another legend is that when Ayyappa entered his teens, he left home on a divine mission to kill Udayanan (a brigand at Sabari hills). He set about gathering followers, appointing the Muslim vavar, a pious Sufi or a medicine man, according to some, as his lieutenant. For Vavar and his fellow Muslim soldiers, Ayyappa arranged for the construction of a mosque at Erumeli.[48]

There are descendants of Vavar living in central Travancore districts. Haji A.R. Vavaru Musaliar of Mallappally Taluk of Pathanamthitta district says:

> I am the 13th descendant of Vavaru. Some people portray him as a fierce warrior, and even worse, a pirate who, after being defeated by Ayyappa and repenting for his past sins, becomes Ayyappa's ally and protector. This is not at all what my forefathers told me. I do not believe this. After all, why is Vavar called Swami by the Hindus? He was a holy man, a Sayyid or a Thangal, as we say in Kerala. Both Vavar and Ayyappa, who were very close friends, followed the same teaching, both practiced yoga and meditation. Yes, they were great yogis. Through yoga they had obtained extraordinary powers, which the populace interpreted as miracles. Their aim, however, was to establish peace

[47] Ibid., p. 63.

[48] Yoginder Sikand, *Sacred Spaces: Exploring Traditions of Shared Faith in India*, New Delhi: Penguin, 2003, pp. 27-28.

in a troubled area. The battles they fought were mostly spiritual battles.[49]

Abdul Karim of Erumeli, who claims to be another descendant of Vavar, offers another version:

> According to Abdul Karim, Vavar was not a Sayyid, but a Wali (a friend of God), in other words, a Sufi Saint. He was reciting his prayers at Erumeli when he met Ayyappa, who had just embarked on his mission to find tigress milk for the Queen. They become close friends. According to Musaliar's wife, each year their cousin, the Vavar musaliar, lent the sacred sword, which his ancestors had inherited from the saint himself.[50]

An old and popular song describes the relationship between Ayyappa and Vavar:

Vavar says to his mother:
Mother, I need a dress and a cap
Need a golden chappal and a golden cane
Need a horse rope, mother
A ship should be built for me, mother
Need to meet my friend
In the fight between the two friends
Ayyappa glitters in the fighting front
Vavar hits Ayyappa with his sword
They fought for seven days and nights

[49] Dominique-Sila Khan, *Sacred Kerala*, p.65.
[50] Ibid., p. 66.

No one wins in the battle

Hearing the clarion call of war Sree Bhagavan appears

You elder and younger brothers must join your hands and speak unitedly
They tie their hands
They roar and go to Sabarimala
Vavar sits here
Friend Ayyappa sits here (Sabarimala).[51]

Ayyappa and Vavar, who fight, are then fast friends. Other myths tell similar stories: Vavar rescued Ayyappa from a demon, after which Ayyappa says to his father, 'Consider Vavar as me.'

But who is Vavar? One legend says that he was a Muslim saint – Hazrath Vavar Baba – who came from Arabia to India to preach Islam. Another says that he was an invader, whose army attacked the king of Pandalam, and Ayyappa was sent to defend the kingdom. Another suggests that Vavar did not come from Arabia but from Tamil Nadu.[52]

> Vavar, or Vavaru Swami as he is sometimes called, is one of the most intriguing figures of Kerala's religious history. If he was, indeed, a friend, or a lieutenant or a disciple of Ayyappa, and if the Sheikh [Fariduddin, Sufi saint who came to Kerala and prayed at Kanjiramattam] was the

[51] V. Krishnakumar, 'Ayyappanum Vavarum Oru Pazhaya Pattu' (Ayyappa and Vavar – an old song), *Mathrubhumi Weekly*, vol. xxxi, 26 April 1953, p. 33.
[52] Khan, *Sacred Kerala*, p. 101.

same as the famous north Indian Muslim saint, then Vavar should have lived in the fourteenth century.[53]

The Presence of Vavar in the history and folklore of Sabarimala Ayyappa shows how syncretic and heterogeneous was this cult in the popular imagination. There are records corroborating the Vavar family's rights in the Sabarimala temple premise entrusted by the Pandalam ruler. 'One of the documents produced before the Kerala High Court by a descendant believed to be of Vavar to establish his right to performance rituals at the shrine of Vavar (Vavarunada) and collection of offerings, dates back to the Malayalam era 884, roughly corresponding to 1708'. Their claim was accepted by the court and they continue their presence at the temple.[54]

The Sabarimala pilgrims still come to Erumeli Vavar's Mosque to offer coconuts before turning to the shrine.

At Sabarimala, there is no idol of Vavar. He is represented by a carved stone slab, a green silk cloth hung on the walls, and an old sword near the wall. Green pepper is offered to this shrine – a nod to the pepper trade that drew him to Kerala. He is also offered rose water, sandalwood paste, coconut, and ghee. What is important to underline is that, in keeping with the prescriptions of Islam, there is no idol here. There is only the aura of Vavar.

[53] Ibid., pp. 61-62.

[54] S.N. Sadasivan, *A Social History of India*, Delhi: APH Publishing, 2000, p. 129.

The Christian Tale

Arthunkal Church is on Kerala's coastline. It is not too far from Kanjirappally, which, legend says, was the home of Vavar. Thousands of pilgrims of all faiths to Sabarimala go to this church as part of their journey and offer their Sabarimala malas (strings of beads) to the church to mark the end of their journey. After the devotees give their malas to the church, they bathe in the church's tank or in the sea. Khan observes that 'Most devotees seem to have no qualms worshiping the white father [Veluthachan], and chant Veluthan Swamiyae Saranamayyappa, Arthungal Palliye Saranamayyappa . . ..'[55] Parish records say that the Arthunkal Church was built by Portuguese missionaries. In 1581, Friar Gasper Pius became its vicar. Three years later, Friar Jacomo Fenicio took over. Friar Fenicio is known as *Arthunkal Veluthachan* ('fair-skinned father'). He installed a statue of St. Sebastian in the church. According to the church's account, Friar Fenicio was a close friend of Ayyappa.[56]

In 1902, a fire damaged the Sabarimala temple. The Travancore King ordered its reconstruction. It was Kochu Thomman, a Christian from Mavelikkara, who took the contract for repairing it; he financed and reconstructed the temple.[57]

[55] Dominique-Sila Khan, *Sacred Kerala*, p. 72.

[56] *Deccan Chronicle*, 6 December 2013.

[57] Annakutty V. Kurian-Findeis, 'Interfaith Relations in the Sociocultural Context of Kerala', in *On World Religions: Diversity, Not Dissension*, ed. Anindita N. Balslev, New Delhi: Sage, 2014, p. 218.

SABARIMALA'S TRANSFORMATION TOWARDS A TEMPLE OF HINDU GRANDEUR

In 1929, Kallaraikkal Krishnan Kartha published *Sri Bhuthanathopakhyanam*, the first printed book on Sabarimala Ayyappa.[58] This Malayalam Kilippattu popularized the story of Ayyappa for the first time in literature. It is based on this work that people began to follow the traditions of the Sabarimala pilgrimage. What is remarkable about this book, based on the nineteenth century Sanskrit text *Bhuthanathopakhyanam*, is that it portrays Ayyappa as fully part of the puranic tradition, regardless of the syncretic traces that make up Sabarimala. This book sets in motion a new vision of both Ayyappa and of Sabarimala. But the book could not do all the work by itself; that required institutional and ideological changes, a broader cultural shift that requires documentation.

A Fire in 1950

In 1950, a fire broke out at the Sabarimala temple. A reporter from *The Hindu* covered the story of what appeared, from the beginning, to be an arson attack. 'The historic temple at Sabarimala,' reported *The Hindu*, 'situated on the wild uninhabited hill on the north-eastern border of Travancore is said to have been the target of a raid recently by some hooligans, who are said to have smashed the idol, looted the temple, and set fire to it'.[59] The government's statement

[58] See Introduction, Vidwan Kurumallur Narayana Pillai, *Sri Bhuthanatha Sarvaswam*, Thrissur: Current Books (republication), 1991.

[59] *The Hindu*, 18 June 1950.

described the damage:

> The *Santhikkaran* who went to the temple on 14 June found the *Sreekovil*, the *mandapam,* and the storeroom destroyed by fire and the idol partly damaged.[60]

The destruction was considerable. Once more, the reporter from *The Hindu* offered a fuller picture:

> The main stone idol was found with its head and hands broken and separated from the body. The broken pieces lay beneath the main body of the image. The right leg too was found broken. While the head of the idol had been knocked off, it is reported that there are axe marks on the door of the temple. The storeroom has been broken into and looted.[61]

The government appointed a Special Investigating Officer, Deputy Inspector General of Police K. Kesava Menon. The enquiry commission reported that 'there were fifteen cut marks of violence on the door leading to the *sreekovil* (sanctum sanctorum), indicating forcible entry into the *sreekovil.* The idol was found broken, the head, left hand palm, and fingers separated. There were cut marks on the face of the idol as well as on the forehead'.[62] 'From the evidence so far available,' wrote the reporter from *The Hindu*, 'there are grounds for the

[60] *The Hindu*, 19 June 1950.

[61] *The Hindu*, 22 June 1950.

[62] K. Kesava Menon, *Sabarimala Temple Arson Case: Enquiry Report*, Trivandrum: Government of Kerala, 1957, p. 1.

inference that the destruction of the sacred temple and the shrine was a deliberate act of vandalism'.[63] The police team concurred, 'There were ample indications of a deliberate act of setting fire to the temple at the scene'.[64]

The Enquiry Report alleged that the attackers could not have been Hindus but might have been Christians. The report is saturated with communal assumptions:

> Whatever might be the feelings of a Hindu towards idol worship, it is doubtful whether any Hindu has broken an idol and set fire to a temple. If he is not an idol worshipper, he may refrain from going to the temple, but he may not break the idol and set fire to the temple. The Hindus have no influence over the area and any party of Hindus cannot get into forests without being noticed by Christians.[65]

K. Kesava Menon, the investigating officer, said in his report that the 'Investigation [has] pointed out the hands [sic] of Christians on circumstantial evidence'.[66]

The police had one witness, Ouseph. He said that he followed a party of *muthalalies* (or rich people), consisting of Karimbanal Kochukunhu Muthalali, Jhnellamittath Kuttiachan, Podimittom Verghese, Karipparambil Devasia, Vadakeparambil Thomman, and Pottamkulam Thomas. This group left Erumeli by jeep and went to Kalaketti. From there,

[63] *The Hindu*, 22 June 1950.

[64] Menon, *Sabarimala Temple Arson Case*, p. 2.

[65] Ibid., p. 4.

[66] Ibid., p. 10.

they went by foot to Kollamuzhi.[67] These rich men then sent their servants into the forest to hunt for them. 'Then,' the police report wrote, 'the *Muthalalies* and he went to Nilakkal in search of a church, which they believed to be existing in Nilakkal'.[68] That was that.

From this, the Enquiry Commission concluded that the muthalalies were behind the incident and that this was a religiously-motivated act.

> The possible conclusion is that these Christian *Muthalalies* were out to do something against the Sabarimala temple, the existence of which they believed to be a menace to their very existence. The movements and activities of Abraham and party and other *Muthalalies* in quest of the church can be believed only as a reconnoitring party for the purpose of hatching a plan to destroy the temple once and once for all. This conclusion is supported from the fact that Vattekkunnel Kunjhupapan and party, Ouseph and party, [and] Kochu and party were all adherents and lieutenants of [the] Karimbanal and Kallivayal families who are the forest kings of northern Travancore. With the active connivance of Paili Kunjhupapan and party, the watchdogs could certainly commit this offence at the bidding of the above landlords.[69]

The conclusion drawn – with communal implications – was making an appeal not to facts, but to 'common sense'. 'It

[67] Ibid., p. 32.
[68] Ibid., p. 33.
[69] Ibid.

is common sense,' Kesava Menon wrote, 'to presume that the temple, with gatherings of large numbers of devotees, was a force not only exhibiting the unity of Hindus but also a check in the gradual absorption of lower caste Hindus into the folds of Christianity, and a check against their conversion'.[70]

Whatever may be the enquiry or actuality, the fire at the temple had a great impact on the subsequent history of the temple.

On 1 July, the Hindu Mahamandal called for a hartal in Thiruvananthapuram against the destruction of the temple.[71] That hartal offered an opportunity to take the cause of Sabarimala to the entire region, and to mobilize sentiment to *create* the consciousness of a Hindu community. A new volunteer organization was set up, on which *The Hindu* reported, comprised of 'well-trained youth devoted to the task of protecting Hindu culture and religious institutions'.[72] The formation of this organization was announced a few days before the hartal inside the compound of the Ayyappa temple in Sabarimala. The new organization was to work under the auspices of the ABASS – a group that has since played a visible role with regard to the temple.

Here is a report from *The Hindu*:

> The General Secretary of Ayyappa Seva Sangham, Trivandram [sic], has issued an appeal to all Hindu devotees to lead [an] austere life for seven days from next Saturday (June 24) and to proceed to the altar of the deity

[70] Ibid., p. 9.

[71] *The Hindu*, 2 July 1950.

[72] *The Hindu*, 27 June 1950.

> at Sabarimala for mass worship on the following Saturday. He has appealed to those devotees who may be unable to do so to suspend all other activities and observe fast and prayers on that day at their respective places to serve as a penance for forgiveness.[73]

The re-installation and purification ceremonies were larger events, using the opportunity to make it into something grander and 'typical'. Significant changes in religious practices and customs took place after the renovation of the temple. High priests from across Kerala – Thazhamon Potti and Puthumana Nambudiripad among others – came to perform the ceremony. So did officials of Hindu organizations from across the region.[74] The ABASS took out an Ayyappa Jyothi across Kerala and Tamil Nadu to generate public enthusiasm for Ayyappa and to set the groundwork for the pilgrimage that would follow. Meanwhile the orthodoxy (certain sections of it anyway) had to come to terms with the fact that the old temple structure did not conform to their traditional rules. As *The Hindu* reported:

> Last week's spoliation of the Sabarimala temple in Travancore is attributable also to the Wrath of Agni, in the opinion of certain orthodox sections. They say, citing the *Sthalapuranam* of the temple, that its destruction by fire had been foretold even while the temple was being built some four centuries back. Raja Rajasekharan of Pantalam, who raised the temple, had installed the Ayyappa idol in

[73] *The Hindu*, 21 June 1950.

[74] Ibid.

Sabari facing south-east [,] the direction of Agni (as a matter of rule all deities are installed in the direction of the east in temples in South India), they claimed.[75]

New Rituals for the Deity

In a 1991 case regarding Sabarimala, the Kerala High Court, in its judgement, noted an important affidavit, about the rituals followed at the temple complex, filed by the TDB that owns the temple. 'The religious practices and customs followed earlier had changed during the last forty years, particularly from 1950, the year in which the renovation of the temple took place after the fire disaster', says the affidavit.[76]

One of the key changes has to do with how Ayyappa is described as a key figure in the history of tantric Hinduism. Sabarimala and Ayyappa gained a new official song, a lullaby (*urakkupattu*) – *Harivarasanam* – which is in Sanskrit. The song is sung at night, as the temple is shut down. As the final verses are sung, the assistant *santhis* (priests) leave the sanctum sanctorum in turn. Only the *melsanthi* (chief priest) remains in the *sreekovil* as the song ends. He extinguishes the lamps one by one and closes the doors for the night after the last lamp is extinguished.

The tradition of the song began with Vadakkathillathu Easwaran Namboothiri, the melsanthi appointed on 13 August 1950.[77] He said that 'the practice of singing the *keerthan* was

[75] *The Hindu*, 27 June 1950.

[76] S. Mahendran vs The Secretary, Travancore Devaswom Board, Thiruvananthapuram, AIR 1993 Ker. 42.

[77] Order number 537, issued by the Travancore Devaswom Board, August

started two or three months after me assuming the post of *Santhikkaran*'.[78] Easwaran Namboothiri's memory of how he started singing the song merits quotation:

> It was me who had started the practice of singing Ayyappa's lullaby, *Harivarasanam*, after the *Athazhapooja* in Sabarimala and *Nadayadakal* by lighting [the] camphor myself and the temple functionaries . . . singing this *Keerthan* as a *Bhajan* after *Athazhapooja*. This *Keerthan* is in *Sasthasthuthi kadambam* published by Kambankudi Sundaram Kulathu Ayyar. A devotee gifted me this book when I was the *Santhi* at Achankovil temple. Before the introduction of this *Keerthan* the former Santhi Chengannur Kuttamani Thirumeni performed the *Nadayadappu* [closing ceremony] by playing the flute.[79]

V.R. Gopala Menon, a devotee of Ayyappa, stayed in Sabarimala when Namboothiri was the melsanthi. He was known by his nickname – *Sabrimalayile kudikidappukaran* (lit., Sabarimala's tenant). A close friend of Easwaran Namboothiri, he used to sing the *Harivarasanam* each day. Gopala Menon died during one of his regular walks in the forest around Sabarimala. Hearing of the death of his friend, Easwaran Namboothiri sang the *Harivarasanam* as he closed the sanctum in honour of Gopala Menon. That is how, it is said, the song is now sung when the sanctum is closed for the

1950.

[78] *Kerala Kaumudi*, 27 December 1995.

[79] *Deshabhimani*, 1 May 2005.

night.[80] The Puranic imprint can be clearly seen in the song:

He is worshipped by the three worlds, is the soul of all gods,
He who is lord Siva, resides in a holy place,
Worshipped three times a day, thing about him itself is fulfilling,
Son of Hari and Hara, I take refuge in thee, O Lord
My refuge is in you Ayyappa, My refuge is in you Ayyappa
He destroys fear, brings prosperity,
He is enchanter of the universe, wears holy ash as ornament,
He rides a white noble elephant,
Son of Hari and Hara, I take refuge in thee, O Lord
My refuge is in you Ayyappa, My refuge is in you Ayyappa
Blessing with an enchanting smile, He has a pretty face,
He is adorned by sandal paste, has a pretty physique,
He rides on royal lion and tiger,
Son of Hari and Hara, I take refuge in thee, O Lord
My refuge is in you Ayyappa,
My refuge is in you Ayyappa
He is dear to his devotees, thought about him itself is fulfilling,
He, who is praised by songs, lives [the] life of ascetics,
He is the essence of hearing sweet music, who enjoys divine music,
Son of Hari and Hara, I take refuge in thee, O Lord
My refuge is in you Ayyappa,
My refuge is in you Ayyappa,
My refuge is in you Ayyappa,

80 *Malayala Manorama*, 10 November 2000.

My refuge is in you Ayyappa,
My refuge is in you Ayyappa[81]

The song describes Ayyappa as Hariharaputhra and as a god glorified by the Vedas. The temple of Sabarimala becomes a temple of OM here. The popularity of this Sanskrit song seals the image of Ayyappa as a legendary Hindu god. The popular notions of Ayyappa as a warrior-god and his other local chronicles, as seen in Ayyappan paattukal is replaced here.

Sabarimala had been a non-sectarian place of worship for years, with people from diverse religious backgrounds coming to pay their respects to the many different divine elements in the temple complex. The Temple Arson Enquiry Report of the fire in 1950, for instance, notes, 'There are examples of non-Hindus offering prayers to cure illness of their children and for better production in agriculture and really offer[ing] prayers and giv[ing] coconuts, ghee and what not, to this forest deity'.[82] Two scholars, writing in the early years of this century, point out that the residue of that ecumenical and progressive spirit remains in small doses: 'Kerala's progressive public discourse since the States Reorganisation Act, 1956, has preferred to represent Sabarimala – where non-Hindus are allowed to participate and where Ayyappa has a Muslim and a "tribal" as helpers – as a truly unique, non-communal religious space expressing an inherent and particularly Malayali egalitarian spirit where everyone is equal as a swami'.[83] But, it needs to be

[81] Suresh Santhikal (ed.), *Sarva Namajapangal*, Cherthala: Sharon Books, 2012, p. 30.

[82] Menon, *Sabarimala Temple Arson Case*, p. 9.

[83] Filippo Osella and Caroline Osella, 'Ayyappan Saranam: Masculinity and the

said that in the past few decades, the number of non-Hindus who have paid a visit to Sabarimala has decreased, and the pilgrimage has become a largely Hindu Affair.

An example of the change in custom at Sabarimala comes in the form of the Erumeli *pettathullal*.[84] Erumeli is a town in Kottayam district that is on the Sabarimala pilgrimage route. The pettathullal, which takes place there, commemorates the killing of Mahishi by Manikanta (or Ayyappa). The pilgrims paint themselves in dots and stripes with ashes, saffron, and carbon. They carry symbolic arrows and clubs, as well as bundles containing fruits and vegetables tied at the top. The *kanni* Ayyappas – the men who are on their first pilgrimage, who must do the pettathullal – lead the way. The pilgrims dance rhythmically to the accompaniment of drums and cymbals. They chant '*Ayyappa thinthakathom, Swami thinthakathom*', an invocation that is supposed to mesmerize the pilgrim with thoughts of Ayyappa. This pettathullal starts from a small Ayyappa shrine at Erumeli and then proceeds to the main temple. As the dancers reach the main temple, branches of trees are thrown on its roof, and the pilgrims attempt to circumambulate the temple. Camphor is burnt before the deity, and the dance ends. There are other pettathullals – from Ambalappuzha and from Alangad, for example, each one bringing large crowds to the main temple. Kurumallur Narayana Pillai, a staunch Ayyappa devotee and one of the earliest authors of Ayyappa books, says about the early 1940s that 'in the old days Erumeli Pettathullal took place on

Sabarimala Pilgrimage in Kerala', *The Journal of the Royal Anthropological Institute*, Vol. 9, no. 4, 2005, pp. 749-750.

[84] A ritualistic dance to celebrate the victory of good over evil.

Dhanu (Malayalam month) 27.' He continues, 'but nowadays Pettatullal is ritualistically held even before Dhanu 20.'[85] For such changes, traditions are flexible!

In 1969, a flagstaff (*dhwajam*) was installed in the complex. The priests introduced the padipooja. They discontinued the practice of breaking eighteen coconuts on the eighteen steps, allowing the coconuts to be broken on a stone below the eighteen sacred steps (pathinettampadi).[86] These changes show that customs are amenable to changes in the temple.

But in the case of menstruation-aged women's entry into Sabarimala, the issue that has come alive in our time, 'customs' are unchangeable for those who want to maintain the status quo. Women between the ages of ten and fifty had been banned from the temple. The Notification by the TDB for a ban was issued in 1955. Rule 3(b) of the Kerala Hindu Places of Public Worship (Authorisation of Entry) Rules, 1965, restricts entry of women at such times when they are not, by custom and usage, allowed to enter temples.[87] The notification by the TDB for a ban was issued only a decade earlier, in 1955. Vidwan Kurumallur Narayana Pillai says that women of all ages entered Sabarimala in the 1940s. His words are direct and unequivocal, 'Women before the age of puberty and women who completed the life cycle of menstruation also constitute the Sabarimala pilgrims. Nowadays, young women are also making the pilgrimage for the Sabarigiri Darshan.'[88] The Kerala High Court took up this issue of women's entry

[85] Narayana Pillai, *Sri Bhuthanatha Sarvaswam*, p. 111.

[86] S. Mahendran v. The Secretary, TDB.

[87] *The Hindu*, 12 April 2016.

[88] Narayana Pillai, *Sri Bhuthanatha Sarvaswam*, p. 111.

into Sabarimala in 1991. The TDB, the custodian of the temple, submitted the following to the High Court:

> Women used to visit the temple. The Maharaja of Travancore, accompanied by the Maharani and the Divan, had visited the temple in the Malayalam year of 1115 (1940 A.D.). Thus, women were not prohibited from entering the Sabarimala temple in the olden days, but women in large numbers were also not found visiting the temple. This was not because of any prohibition imposed by the Hindu religion but because of other non-religious factors.[89]

The argument in the High Court goes further:

> For the last 20 years, women, irrespective of their age, were allowed to visit the temple when it opened for monthly poojas. They were not permitted to enter the temple during the Mandalam, Makaravilakku, and Vishu seasons.

There were many instances of film actresses visiting the temple for shootings and young women visiting for the rice feeding ceremony of their children. But the head priest for decades, Thanthri Sri Neelakandaru, told the Court the opposite. 'He stated that he had intimate connections with that temple even before the reinstallation of the deity in 1950. According to him, women belonging to the age between ten and fifty years were prohibited from entering the temple even before 1950'.[90] The priests emphasized that the concept of

[89] S. Mahendran v. The Secretary, TDB.

[90] Ibid.

devaprasnam – or God's will – justified the restriction of entry of women into Sabarimala. Thanthri Maheshvararu wrote a letter to Kummanam Rajasekharan (state secretary of the Hindu Munnani). According to the High Court record:

> He informed Rajasekharan that permitting women between the age of ten and fifty years would be contrary to the customs of the temple. It was mentioned that it was revealed so in all the *Devaprasnam,* conducted at Sabarimala by well-known astrologers. There cannot thus be two opinions about the practice and usage followed in not permitting women aged more than ten and below fifty to worship at Sabarimala temple.[91]

The evocation of Hindu tantric rites, including the astrological verdict of devaprasnam, moved the High Court of Kerala to place restrictions on the entry of women between the ages of ten and fifty to Sabarimala.[92] The 'tradition' of not permitting women into Sabarimala was strictly observed only after this verdict in 1991.

The legend is that Ayyappa was born to destroy a female demon, a demon who could only be vanquished by a child born of both Siva and Vishnu. When Ayyappa killed her, a beautiful woman emerged from her dead body. She had been cursed to live as a demon, but the killing reversed the curse. She was now free, and asked Ayyappa to marry her.

He refused. He had to go to Sabarimala, he said, to answer the prayers of his devotees. Ayyappa tells her that he will, however,

[91] Ibid.
[92] Ibid.

marry her when the kanni swamis stop coming to Sabarimala. She sits and waits for him at a neighbouring shrine near the main temple. She is worshipped as Malikappurathamma, and Ayyappa, the legend goes, continues as a celibate god.

Historical evidence related to Sabarimala are relatively scant and even more so when one tries to understand the supposedly customary restriction on women's entry. If one accepts the view that Ayyappa is the same as Sastha, then this god cannot be a celibate, according to Hindu Agamas. As explained earlier, in Hindu iconography, Sastha is not celibate but is often seen with his consorts. We have the memoir of B.S. Ward, who surveyed Travancore and reached Sabarimala on 16 December 1818. He says 'it [Chourymallay – British accounts write Sabarimala in this fashion] is much frequented by all classes of people, excepting women of that time of life who have intercourse with men are forbidden the place – old women and girls are not debarred'.[93]

From which period this practice originated is not known. The Tantric texts in Kerala don't restrict entry for women, except during the monthly menses cycle. Menstruating women, however, are allowed to visit Sastha temples. Anyhow, this practice should be sociologically analyzed in isolation and in comparison with some practices among Ullatans and Mala Arayas.

L.A. Krishna Iyer notes that 'They [Ullatans] lead a celibate life from December to April because the hill deities and Sastha will otherwise be offended'. This is the same period

[93] B.S. Ward, *Memoir of the Survey of Travancore and Cochin 1816-1820*, Govt. Press, Madras, 1891, p. 70.

when the Makaravilakku festival (in January) takes place in Sabarimala.[94]

Among Mala Arayas there is a practice that 'if the men observe any vow at home, she remains in the shed for seven days. It is feared that the sylvan deities will be offended by allowing her to come earlier, as she may be unclean'. From this, we can infer that the practice of abstinence by these hill men is out of fear of not only Ayyappa but also their other hill deities. Today, the idea of Ayyappa as a Naishtika Brahmachari (celibate god) dominates religious narrative and justifies the restriction on women's entry (although lifted by the Supreme Court), transforming the temple into a space of Hindu masculinity.[95]

A Divine Attraction?

What to make of Makaravilakku, the phenomenon of the 'divine light'? It is the main draw for the pilgrimage that takes place during the forty-one days of the Mandala period that begins on the first day of the Malayalam month of Vrischikam. When the forty-one days end, the temple closes for five days. During this five-day hiatus, no pooja (worship) is conducted. Ayyappa, it is said, is resting after the forty-one days of giving darsan (divine gaze). The temple then opens for another three weeks, and the culmination of the festival season begins after fourteen days. This is known as Makaravilakku or the

[94] L.A. Krishna Iyer, *Travancore Tribes and Castes*, Vol 2, Govt. Press, Trivandrum, 1939, pp. 213.

[95] L.A. Krishna Iyer, *Travancore Tribes and Castes*, Vol 1, Govt. Press, Trivandrum, 1937, p 178.

Makaram lights. Two religious studies scholars describe what happens next:

> On the first day of the Malayalam month of Makaram (from mid-January to mid-February), a movable image of Ayyappa is enthroned on an elephant and taken in procession to the Pamba river where an Arat (holy bath) is performed. Once bathed, the image is conveyed once more to receive Thiruvabharanam (divine gold ornaments), which arrive in another procession from the town of Pandalam, which is the seat of the Ayyappa's adoptive father, the erstwhile Pandalam Raja. (During this period the temple is closed and the sanctum sanctorum purified.) Huge crowds of pilgrims accompany the procession up into the mountain from Pandalam, together with two divine eagles, which are said to circle the sky for the duration of the journey. The gold ornaments are then taken to the temple and placed on Ayyappa's main image. The principal shrine is closed while the chief priest and his assistants perform Poojas. While the doors of the main shrine are still closed, a bright light appears on top of one of the hills surrounding the temple and a bright star appears in the sky, signs indicating the presence and satisfaction of Ayyappa.[96]

When the bright star appears, the doors of the main shrine open, as the priests perform *deeparadhana* (the circling of the holy flame in front of the deity, which concludes every act of

[96] Osella and Osella, 'Ayyappan Saranam', p. 732.

pooja), the light in the sky disappears.

In 2015, a reporter from *The Hindu*, Radhakrishnan Kuttoor, covered the festival and wrote about how the pilgrims experienced this incredible event. He wrote:

> With hardly twenty-six hours for the Makaravilakku festival, the Sabarimala Sannidhanam is overflowing with Ayyappa devotees from different parts of the country. For the past two days, scores of pilgrims are camping in the forests to worship the Makarajyoti, a celestial star that appears on the eastern horizon of the Sannidhanam coinciding with the Deeparadhana at the temple, and the Makaravilakku atop the Ponnambalamedu facing the Ayyappa temple, on Wednesday evening. Many devotees were seen perched on trees and rooftops, though there were restrictions, from where they could worship the Makaravilakku. Pilgrims in large numbers were camping in makeshift shelters on hillsides in the surrounding forests to worship the Makarajyoti.[97]

There is a fierce debate over the question of Makaravilakku, namely, is the divine light in fact 'divine' or is it man-made? The most important element to remember is that the pilgrimage to Sabarimala is also defined around the light that is believed to be a miracle. It is believed by lakhs of pilgrims that the light appears miraculously at Ponnambalamedu (the abode of Ayyappa) and that it is the celestial manifestation of the god Ayyappa. Others, who nonetheless believe it is a miracle, say it

[97] *The Hindu*, 14 January 2015.

is not Ayyappa himself, but an aarthi performed by the rishis and devas living in the hills. Even the media seems to broadcast its miraculous nature without any real investigation. *The New Indian Express*, in 2008, suggested that there are two events that 'evade scientific explanation – just before the Vilakku appears, a star rises in the sky and a kite hovers over the temple.'[98] On a live television show at the Makaravilakku, one of the reporters breathlessly said, 'There it rises, the Makara Jyothi; first as a lightning, then as a lamp or star as camphor light . . . there it rises, disappears, and then appears again.'[99] Little wonder that the press does not investigate this phenomenon. Stories spread that the Ponnambalamedu is inaccessible to humans and that if people try to reach the origin of the light, they will meet a miserable end.

But the evidence tells us something entirely different. For one, there was no regular light of this kind in the last part of the 1940s or before. Our primary source from this period, the text by Kurumallur Narayana Pillai, describes the 'Makaravilakku from the Manimandapam of Malikappuram to the holy 18th step in the night of the day of Makarasankramam.'[100] He suggests that the lights from the hills are not a regular phenomenon. His sincere description is worth reading in full:

> Devotees believe that Devathas and Rishis perform Deeparadhana at Ponnambalamedu at the same time when Deeparadhana is conducted in Sannidhanam. It is

[98] *The New Indian Express*, 29 May 2008.

[99] Translation of a live Malayalam commentary aired on Aakashvani, 14 January 1981.

[100] Narayana Pillai, *Sri Bhuthanatha Sarvaswam*, p. 153.

> with this belief that devotees turn to the north side and pray by joining their hands before God. In some years there used to be the appearance of a light from the hills of [the] northern side. Devotees believe that it is a Vilakku in Ponnambalamedu.[101]

Not every year, but in some years, there used to be the appearance of a light from the hills of the northern side. No newspapers of the year after the arson at Sabarimala temple (when *The Hindu* and *Malayala Rajyam* covered the temple activities at length) mention the Makaravilakku Darsan (here, Makaravilakku is used to denote the light from Ponnambalamedu only; not to be confused with the ritual) as an important phenomenon. One can only surmise that the Makaravilakku lights, as an intrinsic phenomenon, is a later development and provided a greater impetus for the increased popularity of the pilgrimage and for Sabarimala's transformation into a famous pilgrim centre.

Several times over the past few decades, rationalists and honest officials have admitted that the Makaravilakku is in fact, man-made. This was later admitted by the TDB and Tantri himself. The first serious effort to enquire whether it was man-made took place due to the initiative of the Kerala Yukthivadi Sangham ('atheist association') in 1981. A busload of activists from the Association arrived at Ponnambalamedu on 14 January 1981. When the authorities lit the camphor and raised the flame thrice facing Sabarimala, the rationalist activists lit their firecrackers and began filming the episode. The radio

[101] Ibid., p. 149.

commentators and reporters of newspapers, clueless about the presence of the rationalists, faithfully reproduced the official story. 'Makara Jyothis appeared,' reported *Mathrubhumi*, 'not once, but many times.'[102] 'Next to the Jyothy, there also appeared a number of small lights,' said *Deepika*.[103] Amongst the rationalists was A.V. Jose, who later wrote about his findings in *Yukthivicharam*:

> The information we have is that before the officials of KSEB (Kerala State Electricity Board) and Pampa Irrigation Project arrived at Ponnambalamedu, the tribal people belonging to the Katar and Mala Araya tribes used to live there. To protect themselves from the extreme cold of the December–January winter as well as to cook food, they might have lit fire in the evenings. Devotees visiting Sabarimala during Makaravilakku season might have taken such a fire to be a 'divine light' and started worshipping it as Makarajyothi. They might not have observed whether this light had been there before and the day after Makarasankranthi. When the Pampa irrigation project was implemented, the tribal people left the hills. The Devaswom authorities, who wanted to use it to defraud the pilgrims, however, have made a permanent arrangement to light this 'divine light' on the day of Makarasankranthi.[104]

[102] *Mathrubhumi*, 15 January 1981.

[103] *Deepika*, 15 January 1981.

[104] A.V. Jose, 'Makaravilakku Enna Thattippu' (Makaravilakku as a hoax), Yukthivicharam, February 1981.

Two decades later, the former president of the TDB Raman Nair said that 'the Makaravilakku is also done with the help of the police and other people'.[105]

In January 2011, after the Makaravilakku, as the pilgrims descended the hill, a car blocked their way, which caused a major stampede. About 106 people died. Asked about the Makaravilakku, the senior thanthri Kandararu Maheswararu said, 'Makarajyothi is a star in the sky and Makaravilakku was a traditional Deeparadhana at Ponnambalamedu'. But then, he also hedged his views, 'The Jyothi is a celestial phenomenon, but the Vilakku is a fire lit for the Deeparadhana by people. In the past, tribal families used to light this fire'.[106] The Thanthri did not talk about details of these 'people', not the 'tribal families' who lit the fire 'in the past', but the 'people' who light it now.

The former commissioner of the TDB from 2008 to 2011, P.V. Nalinakshan Nair, wrote a letter to Justice (Retd.) R. Bhaskaran, the ombudsman for the Travancore and Cochin Devaswom Boards.[107] He said that the lighting in Ponnambalamedu has a history of nearly forty-five years. Who lit the lamps? This man, who had been in charge of TDB, and therefore of Sabarimala too, said of the lighting:

> The lighting had originally been done by a few families of the Malayaraya [sic] tribe. Officers attached to the Kerala State Electricity Board continued the practice when the forest-dwellers were evicted in connection with the

105 *DNA*, 30 May 2008.

106 *The Hindu*, 24 January 2011.

107 *The Hindu*, 23 January 2011.

The Sabarimala temple complex (circled) is across the valley, seen from Ponnambalamedu, a hill-top east of the Sannidhanam. The cement platform, where the fire is lit, was built by the Travancore Devaswom Board in the 1990s. Source: *The Hindu*.

> Sabarigiri Hydro-electric Project. The TDB and the Police department took over the duty when the KSEB official[s] left the place at a later time.

'The executive engineer of the TDB at Pamba was in charge of arranging the lights' he says. Nair was the former additional commissioner of income tax, so what bothered him was that the expenses of the TDB had not been debited. It was that which irked him enough to write the letter to Bhaskaran. Why was it necessary for the TDB and the KSEB to turn on the light? The jyothi, he wrote, was a 'signal to disperse the crowd according to the officials'. Then, he continued:

> The officers were trying to make a necessity out of a blatant falsehood. When it dawned on me that the Devaswom

> will never have the will to abandon the practice, I suggested that the Board should at least make it legitimate by incorporating it as a Devaswom ritual, for which expenditure could be debited in the Devaswom accounts and in course of time declare Makarajyothi as a Devaswom ritual. My suggestion fell on deaf ears and I left it at that.[108]

Because of the stampede, he told *The Hindu*, the 'fraud has become a crime'. Why did he come forward at this time and not while he was the commissioner of the TDB? The death of over a hundred people, 'the spectral images of the bodies with tenuous spasm[s] of life, thrown together and carted off like carcasses, linger in my thoughts and hound me as a nightmare', he said.

Most importantly, Pandalam royal authorities, erstwhile custodians of the temple, have said that the lighting at Ponnambalamedu is a relatively new practice and does not have an ancient or divine origin. The Pandalam Palace Managing Committee president, P. Rama Varma Raja, said forthrightly:

> The Pandalam Palace does not give any importance to the Makarajyothi at Ponnambalamedu, which was the creation of certain vested interests with a hidden agenda to downplay the most important event of Deeparadhana offered to the deity decorated with the sacred Thiruvabharanam [sacred ornaments] brought from the Pandalam Palace, on Makaravilakku day. Vilakku is an old

[108] *The Hindu*, 23 January 2011.

Malayalam usage for a temple festival, and Makaravilakku is referred to [as] the temple festival at Sabarimala on the day of MakaraSankramam.[109]

Amid this debate, on 21 January 2011, *The Hindu* printed a photograph taken in 2006 of the place where the fire is lit for the Makaravilakku. This was fairly conclusive evidence of how the lights appeared. But it has not shaken the view of many pilgrims and devotees, who continue to say that the lights are divine or are lit by sages.

Officials in Kerala, whether in the government or in the temple administration, now admit that the Adivasis used to light the fire, performing deeparadhana at Ponnambalamedu. The TDB filed an affidavit with the Kerala High Court in 2011that said that the Makaravilakku was lit by Adivasis in the forest. The High Court's reaction is of interest. It said that the TDB could henceforth send its own priest to light the fires.[110]

The High Court's position has not satisfied the Adivasi communities, such as the Mala Araya community, which had performed the deeparadhana ritual at Ponnambalamedu in older days. Their demand was that they must be given the right to perform the ritual. Thanthri Kandararu Maheswararu endorsed the views of the Mala Araya community regarding Makaravilakku. He suggested that 'Travancore Devaswom Board should include two members of the Mala Araya community and one priest on the team to perform the Makaravilakku ritual. There was even a sentiment that the presence of the Mala Araya members would make the ritual

[109] *The Hindu*, 21 January 2011.

[110] *The Times of India*, 30 April 2011.

more sacred'.[111] The president of Travancore Devaswom Board, Rajagopalan Nair, and the Visakham Thirunal Rama Varma Raja, the head of the royal family of Pandalam, said that they had no objection to Mala Araya cooperation in this ritual. Fascinatingly, this is also part and parcel of the pan-India attempt to incorporate Adivasis into the fabric of neo-Hinduism.

Reconstructing the Temple

The arson of 1950 was followed by a renovation of the Sabarimala temple. Ayyappa's old image, made of stone, was badly damaged in the fire of 1950. The new deity was installed following all the strict Hindu tantric rituals. The Brahmin astrologer, Kanipayyur Sankaran Namboodiripad, set the time for the installation. Thanthri Thazhamon Kandararu provided the auspicious time from Kanippayyur for the making of the panchaloha Ayyappa. The idol was created in the *uttupura* (dining hall) of Chengannur Mahakshethram by Chengannur Ayyappan Asari and his team. The *punaprathishta* (reinstallation) took place on Atham Nakshathram, on the 4th of the Malayalam month of Edavam, after which the more conventional rituals, such as *padipooja* and *uthradam sadhya,* became key to the worship.[112]

The changes related with the presence of Vavaruswami Nada in Sabarimala are important to be noted. The presence of a shrine to a Muslim man – Vavar – as part of the Ayyappa tradition and within Sabarimala is one of the most illustrious

[111] *The Times of India*, 30 April 2011.

[112] *Deshabhimani*, 1 May 2005.

examples of our shared culture. Earlier, the shrine to Vavar was just below the eighteenth step in Sabarimala. The installation of the Vavar in Sabarimala was renovated after 1905 (the Malayalam year 1080). Vidwan Kurumallur Narayana Pillai says that 'There was an order from Hajoor on 1080 Medam 20100 to prepare an expenditure estimate for the renovated installation to Vavarswami in Vavarunada in Sabarimala'. The temple priests never denied the shrine to Vavar. [113] The temple priests never denied the shrine to Vavar. According to Narayana Pillai's records 'in the Malayalam year 1089', Thazhamon Krishnaru Thanthri wrote that 'there was a Vavar installation and a Vavar temple in the Sabarimala temple premise'.[114] Down the hill, in Erumeli, there is a Vavar *palli* (mosque), which is part of the pilgrimage route on the way to Sabarimala. The pilgrims climbed to Sabarimala and paid their respects to the Vavar shrine in the Sabarimala complex.

In the second half of the twentieth century, Courts accepted the rights of the descendants of Vavar in Sabarimala, based on some historical documents they produced in court, to receive offerings. Today there is Vavarunada in Sabarimala, below the eighteen steps, a distance away. The story of the relation between Ayyappa and Vavar is not obliterated yet, but there are attempts to portray Vavar as Vaparan, not a Muslim, belonging to Boothagana.

Sabarimala Ayyappa had become a typical Hindu tantric god and had gradually lost his heterodox roots.

[113] Narayana Pillai, *Sri Bhuthanatha Sarvaswam*, p. 215.

[114] Ibid., p. 216.

THE NILAKKAL CRUCIBLE

In 1983, a dispute occurred around the discovery of a cross near the Mahadeva temple in Nilakkal, a little over twenty kilometres from Sabarimala. The Nilakkal area is sacred terrain to both Christians and Hindus and is claimed by both. Christians believe that it was in the Nilakkal area that St. Thomas, one of the apostles of Christ, built a church shortly after arriving in Kerala. Joseph Pulikkunnel, a Christian theologian, said that Nilakkal is the religious heritage of all Christian denominations in Kerala.[115] The Hindus believe that Nilakkal is part of the Poonkavanam of Sabarimala Ayyappa. Both see the area as sacred and, indeed, for a very long period, there was no need for either to contest the sensibilities of each other. Both religious communities enjoyed their ability to overlap in the area. This comity would be deeply threatened in 1983.

St. Thomas and the Nilakkal church

St. Thomas, it is believed by many Christians, landed at Kodungallur (Kerala) in 52 CE.[116] It is claimed that he established seven and a half churches ('*Ezhara Pallikal*') in Kerala. One of these churches was in Nilakkal, while the others were in Kollam, Palayoor, Kottakkavu, Niranam, Kodungallur, Kokkamangalam, and the church in Thiruvithamcode, which

[115] Joseph Pulikkunnel, 'Nilakkal Prasnam' [The Nilakkal Question], *Yukthivadi*, vol. 54, June 1983, p. 405.

[116] Scholarly consensus on the story of the arrival of St. Thomas in Kerala and the churches he built is not settled.

is known as Arappalli (Half Church).[117] M.C. Joseph, the former president of the Kerala Catholic Congress, said during the fracas in 1983 that Nilakkal is one of the most important places for Kerala's ancient Christian religion. The *Marthoma Charithram*, which narrates the Evangelical activities of St. Thomas, observes that he visited Nilakkal twice. 'The story is that Nilakkal Church, founded by St. Thomas, was destroyed, and ceased to exist due to the attack of Malik Kafur in the 14th century.'[118]

'Records show that in 1902 what was believed to be the remains of the ancient Christian church and cemetery [were] accidentally discovered in the forest regions to the south of the Western Ghats, on the road to the ancient Hindu shrine of Sabarimala in the practically inaccessible mountain recesses,' said Kerala's leading Christian priest Paulos Mar Gregorios. Pulikkottil Joseph Mar Dionysius, the Malankara Metropolitan in 1902, wrote to K. Krishnaswamy Rao, the Dewan of Travancore, to say that 'this was one of the seven churches established by St. Thomas, that the British Resident had promised Rs. 20,000 to build the church on that site.' The Metropolitan told the Dewan to convince him that the church was needed to establish a settlement in Nilakkal and it would assist 'the thousands of Hindu devotees who annually repair to the forest temple' of Sabarimala. His petition was not acted upon.

According to Gregorios, 'in the late 1930s or early 1940s, an Orthodox man who worked in the Forest Department of the Government of Travancore discovered the site once more.

[117] *Kerala Kaumudi*, 12 April 1983; *Deepika*, 11 April 1983.

[118] *Kerala Kaumudi*, 12 April 1983.

He found a bell and a large cross there. The Church appealed to C.P. Ramaswami Iyer, the Dewan of Travancore, to endow the land for the rebuilding of a church. The Dewan refused. He had the bell and cross removed.'[119]

A decade later, in February 1957, a priest of the Orthodox Church found what he claimed to be the basement of the ancient Church as well as several graves.

Whatever might be the truth behind these numerous incidents of discovery of church remains, it is an indisputable fact that the demand for a church at Nilakkal was years old.

Ayyappa and his Poonkavanam

It is said that Nilakkal is within Ayyappa's Poonkavanam, 'a symbolic territory in the form of an envelope crowning the Sabarimala temple or immediate sphere of influence of the deity (Sabarimala Kshetram)', which consists of the eighteen hills that surround the Sabarimala temple.[120] The eighteen hills are Sabarimala, Ponnambalamedu, Gaundan Mala, Naga Mala, Sundara Mala, Chuttambalamedu, Mathanga Mala, Mayiladummedu, Sreepada Mala, Devar Mala, Nilakkal Mala, Thalappara Mala, Neeli Mala, Kari Mala, Puthusseri Mala, Kalaketti Mala, Injipara Mala, and Kalki Mala. Rémy Delage, who has studied Sabarimala, says that even if these hills can be located on a map – see below – '*Poonkavanam* is a symbolic

[119] Paulos Mar Gregorios, 'Communal Violence in Kerala', *The Star of the East*, September 1983.

[120] Christophe Z. Guilmoto, Sebastian Oliveau, Virginie Chasles, Rémy Delage, and Stephanie Vella, 'Mapping out Social Change in South India. A Geographic Information System and its Applications', *Pondy Papers in Social Sciences*, Institut Français de Pondichéry, 2004, p. 40.

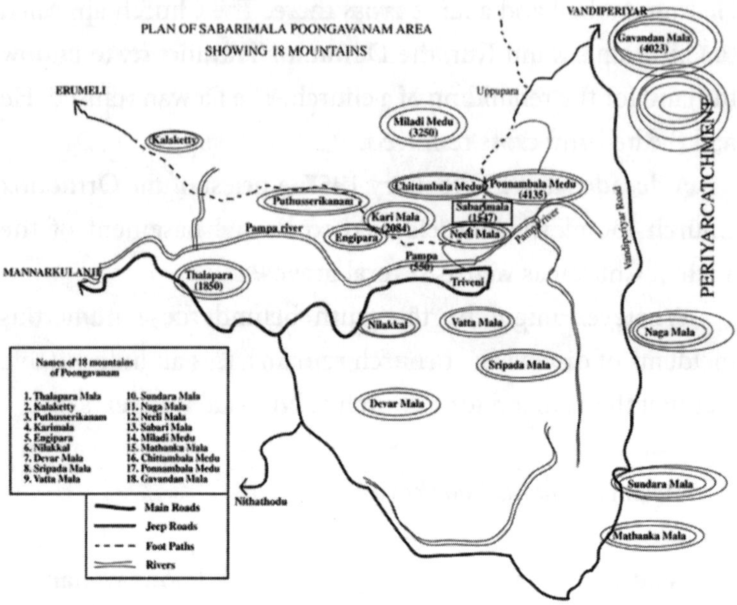

Source: *A Book on Ayyappa Mahatmyam and Vana Yatra (Malayalam) (A book on Sabarimala Pilgrimage and Forest Trek)*

Map of the Poonkavanam. See Guilmoto et al., 'Mapping out Social Change in South India. A Geographic Information System and its Applications', p. 49.

territory'.[121] It should not be mistaken as mapped onto the world that can be walked.

Only in 1983 did the claim of Ayyappa's Poonkavanam become a matter of public awareness and dispute. Pavanan, in a magazine article, offers the correct breathless tone for the 'discovery':

> A new story has come out related to the Nilakkal *issue*. It

[121] Rémy Delage, 'Beyond Territory: The Process of Geographical Identification in the Context of a South Indian Pilgrimage', unpublished paper submitted to Association Jeunes Études Indiennes, p. 6 (https://ajei.hypotheses.org/files/2013/01/AJC03-delage.pdf, last accessed 19 March 2020).

is that Ayyappa has a *Poonkavanam*. The Hindu saints are arguing that no Christian church should be built in any part of the *Poonkavanam* of Sabarimala Ayyappa.[122]The Hindu orthodox leadership received support from the family of the Pandalam Palace, the heirs of the Pandalam Raja. Given the belief that Ayyappa is the adopted son of the Pandalam Raja, the words of the Pandalam Palace were taken seriously. Historically Pandalam had rights over the Sabarimala and surrounding forest regions before they went for the Pandalam Adamanam (discussed earlier) and later annexation with Travancore state. According to them, 'The entire 3,000 hectares of forest area known as the Poonkavanam of Lord Ayyappa was under the possession of the royal family of Pandalam before being taken over during the British Raj'.[123] P. Kerala Varma Raja of the Pandalam Palace oversaw mapping the eighteen hills and streams that he claimed made up the actual Poonkavanam.[124] The result of these efforts was that the clerics and the Pandalam Palace were able to establish geography for the Poonkavanam and, consequently, to claim the entire Nilakkal region as part of the sacred space of Ayyappa.

[122] 'Pavanan, 'Prathimasa Rekhakal' [Monthly Documents], *Yukthirekha*, Book. 1, September 1983, p. 14.

[123] *The Hindu* Business Line, 21 June 2005.

[124] Kummanam Rajasekharan, 'Ajatha Sathruvaya Kerala Varma Raja' [King Kerala Varma, the 'One Without an Enemy'], *Kesari*, 11 July 2010, p. 44.

Discovery of the Cross

On 25 March 1983, the newspaper *Deepika* ran a story about the discovery of a granite cross by workers on government-owned Farming Corporation land at Nilakkal. The paper, which was owned by the Syrian Church, carried a photograph of the cross.[125] The discovery took place between Plapalli and Chalakkayam, about twenty kilometres from Sabarimala.[126] Workers told the priest of the nearby Thulappalli St. George Church, who then led a prayer for the discovery. Within two days, the cross, which many believers thought 'belonged' to the time of St. Thomas and was claimed as such, vanished from the site.[127]

Christian devotees came to see the cross. Religious services began. Fifteen priests offered *samoohabali* at the site.[128] Four to five times a day, the priests condu cted services at a temporary church. They drew the boundaries of the church by walling in two acres of forest land.[129] Church authorities said that they would continue to hold prayers for thousands of people until the cross was recovered. Along the road to Nilakkal, billboards appeared with signs for St. Thomas Road. The Church authorities wanted to build a permanent church at the site.

Questions were raised about the myth of St. Thomas's cross. A fact-finding team visited the site. Its members were respected historians and theologians – Kerala Catholic

[125] *Deepika*, 25 March 1983.

[126] Editorial, *Kerala Kaumudi*, 14 April 1983.

[127] *Deepika*, 29 March 1983.

[128] *Deepika*, 11 April 1983. Samoohabali refers to the concelebration of the Holy Eucharist.

[129] *Mathrubhumi*, 15 April 1983.

Almaya Association General Secretary Joseph Pulikkunnel, Kerala History Congress President N.K. Jose, archaeologist John Ochanthuruthu, and the publisher D.C. Kizhakemuri. After they visited Nilakkal and studied the situation (without access to the cross itself), they said that the cross discovered would not be a Mar Thoma Cross. They said that there is no record in the history of Christianity, from any part of the world, which shows reverence to a cross in the first century when St. Thomas is believed to have come to Kerala. Joseph Pulikkunnel said that in the early days the religious symbol of Christianity was not the cross, but the fish.[130] The granite crosses discovered in different parts of Kerala are not older than the eighth century CE. For that reason, the cross could not be from the time of St. Thomas.[131] Pulikkunnel said that the cross discovered in Nilakkal was not shaped like very ancient crosses. It was similar, he said, to the shape of the modern Roman cross.[132] This debate did not assuage believers, who continued to feel that this was St. Thomas's cross and that the church must nonetheless be built there.

The cross had been found only two hundred metres from the Nilakkal Mahadeva temple, a Siva temple. The TDB president, T.N. Upendranath, said that he would not permit a church to be built in that area. Mobilizations began not mainly as a drive to protect the Nilakkal Mahadeva temple, only two hundred metres away but to campaign to protect the Sabarimala temple, which was more than twenty kilometres away. The idea that the church would impinge on Ayyappa's

[130] Pulikkunnel, 'Nilakkal Prasnam', p. 406.

[131] *Kerala Kaumudi*, 30 April 1983.

[132] Pulikkunnel, 'Nilakkal Prasnam', pp. 406–7.

Poonkavanam became the main focus. The symbolic value of the Poonkavanam created the basis for a very real Hindu unity campaign.

Defend Sabarimala

Rather than a sober discussion, the immediate reaction from the Hindu organizations was that this was an assault on the integrity of Ayyappa and a shadow conspiracy against the Sabarimala temple. Such a view spread across Kerala, helping the orthodox sections to mobilize support to 'defend Sabarimala'.

These protesting organizations included two familiar bodies, both local, the TDB and ABASS, a caste organization (NSS), and organizations on the hard right (RSS, Vishwa Hindu Parishad (VHP), and the Hindu Munnani). The NSS general secretary, Kidangoor Gopalakrishna Pillai, told the press at Kottayam that his organization and the others would not give up their fight:

> Encroachers must be considered as such and evicted. There is no question of settlement in this matter. Hindus are not ready for any compromise. [If a] Cross is installed within two hundred metres of the premise of the ancient Nilakkal temple, this act would cause to deteriorate the existing religious harmony.[133]

At a meeting of various Hindu organizations in

[133] *Mathrubhumi*, 18 April 1983.

Thiruvananthapuram, they decided to make this a Kerala-wide issue. The organizations named above were joined by the Rama Dasa Mission, the Chinmaya Mission, the Hindu Mission, and the Visala Hindu Sammelan.[134] They decided to observe 30 April as Nilakkal Day to demand the removal of the temporary church. They said that the government must evict the church from the Farming Corporation land.[135] At the meeting, the group formed the Nilakkal Action Council with a president (Swami Sathyananda Saraswathi) and a general convenor (Kummanam Rajasekharan).[136] Swami Sathyananda Saraswathi would later be a key person in the Rath Yathra across southern India for the building of a Ram temple at the site of the Babri Masjid (1989-92) and in the 'Guruvayoor Temple Liberation Struggle' (1996). Kummanam Rajasekharan, meanwhile, began his political career in the RSS and would later (2015-18) become the state president of BJP. Both men are politically right-wing, which defined the character of the Nilakkal Action Council.

The church authorities declined to accept the view that their church would insult the religious sentiments of devout Hindus at the Nilakkal temple. All-Kerala Catholic Congress President and the Nilakkal Church Action Committee Convenor Joseph Manniparambil said that the church 'doesn't pose any disturbance or threat to the Mahadevar temple or the religious activities there'.[137] It was, indeed, the view of the TDB President to portray the church as an attack against the Hindu

[134] *Mathrubhumi*, 21 April 1983.
[135] *Mathrubhumi*, 25 April 1983.
[136] *Mathrubhumi*, 24 April 1983.
[137] Ibid.

temple that was provocative, he added. The Nilakkal Action Council decided to conduct statewide protest marches and public meetings on its self-fashioned Nilakkal Day. Saffron flags were to be unfurled, and protest boards displayed at temples and public places.[138] A caravan of sanyasins planned to go to Nilakkal on 27 April, three days before Nilakkal Day. The Sangh Parivar, not active in Kerala in 1950 when the fire broke out in Sabarimala, had, by this time, developed a network across the state. RSS became the leader of this struggle. 'Up to that period,' wrote Joseph Pulikkunnel, 'the presence of the RSS was almost unknown.'[139] The Akhil Bharatiya Karyakarini Mandal (ABKM) – the RSS's all-India executive council – passed several resolutions on the issue of Nilakkal. The one below illustrates the attitude of the RSS and the Sangh Parivar in general:

> ABKM considers it most unfortunate that some fanatical sections of Christians have trespassed into and set up a church at Nilakkal – a sacred spot of pilgrimage for the entire Hindu people. Such a church within the eighteen holy hills complex of the famous Sabarimala Temple would obviously prove to be a constant source of pain for the Hindu religious sentiments. The illegal planting of a cross all of a sudden and its equally mysterious disappearance three days later, the application of political pressure on the Government, and the Government's partisan and ill-conceived decision to bow to their demand for a church,

138 Ibid.

139 Joseph Pulikkunnel, 'Nhan RSS?' (Am I RSS?), Osana; republished in *Kesari*, vol. 16, 17 April 2011, p. 29.

> where not a single Christian life is anywhere nearby, these have only further aggravated the situation and severely disturbed the traditional social amity among the different sections of the people of Kerala.[140]

The heat from the RSS began to rise. The K. Karunakaran-led government decided to remove the cross and temporary shed from the close vicinity of the Nilakkal Mahadeva temple and also decided to allot land elsewhere for the building of a church.[141] But this was not acceptable to the RSS and its friends. 'The government decision to allot land for the Church in Nilakkal is unilateral and an act of direct justification of the occupation of public land', they said. 'The Hindu organizations reject this government decision.' The Nilakkal Action Council leaders, men from the Sangh Parivar groups, spoke in the name of *all* Hindus, 'This decision is not acceptable to the Hindus of Kerala.'[142] The situation gradually deteriorated, and the communal spirit was aflame. Mass mobilizations were organized across the state to 'defend' Sabarimala and Ayyappa's Poonkavanam. It was decided to create an 'army' of volunteers numbering more than one lakh people, who were to be ready 'for any sacrifice to protect Hindu interests'.[143] Swami Sathyananda Saraswathi of the Nilakkal Action Council claimed that people were 'envious' of the 'awakening of Hindus'. He demanded that all Hindus 'must unite and

140 *RSS Resolves, 1950–2007: Resolutions Passed by ABPS and ABKM of the RSS from 1950–2007*, New Delhi: Suruchi Prakashan, 2007, pp. 115-116.

141 *Mathrubhumi*, 29 April 1983.

142 *Mathrubhumi*, 30 April 1983.

143 *Mathrubhumi*, 4 May 1983.

Church built at Nilakkal on 28 May 1983. Source: *Kalakaumudi*, 19 June 1983.

organize against the attempt to convert Ayyappa's

Poonkavanam, which represents the culture of spirituality, into a symbol of funeral culture.'[144]

Protection of Sabarimala was the war cry. Years later, Kummanam Rajasekharan of the RSS and the Nilakkal Action Council said that 'the symbolic power of saying that this was an attack on Sabarimala helped unite large numbers of Ayyappa and Hindu devotees. The attempt to build the church was an indirect attack on Nilakkal, which occupies an important place for Sabarimala.'[145] Ayyappa Seva Sangham President D. Damodaran Potti, a former speaker of the Kerala Assembly, said that the pilgrimages to Sabarimala must be used to

144 *Kerala Kaumudi*, 4 May 1983.

145 Interview with Kummanam Rajasekharan, Janam TV (https://youtu.be/mhexazS8Xow, last accessed 26 October 2020).

'discourage the efforts of building a Christian Church near to Nilakkal'.[146] He called upon the *Dharma Bhatans* or 'Moral Soldiers' of the ABASS to protect the Sabarimala Sannidhanam and the Nilakkal temple in Ayyappa's Poonkavanam.[147] P. Parameswaran, an RSS ideologue, called for a special pilgrimage to Nilakkal during the pilgrimage to Sabarimala.[148]

Rumours and provocations of all kinds muddied the water. The Council leaders began to differentiate between the Vavar shrine in Sabarimala and the church in Nilakkal. Their logic was that no Muslims went to pray at Vavar Nada, while Christians wished to pray at Nilakkal Church. This was, to them, unacceptable.[149]

By mid-May 1983, the agitation had become widespread. The Nilakkal Action Council approached the central government to see if it would turn the forest lands into a national pilgrimage centre. This was a canny move, based on their judgement that such constructions cannot be allowed in any part of the Poonkavanam.[150] A few days later, the government said that it had allotted land for the church 325 metres away from the Nilakkal temple.[151] Two days later – on 28 May 1983, around 150 people led by Fr. Antony Nirappel and Fr. Mathew Anthiyakulam reached Nilakkal with lorries carrying building material. A black cross with a crucified Christ was installed on a newly-built stone altar, six feet high and 250 kilograms in weight. A picture of St. Thomas and a

[146] *Mathrubhumi*, 9 May 1983.
[147] *Mathrubhumi*, 10 May 1983.
[148] *Mathrubhumi*, 16 May 1983.
[149] *Mathrubhumi*, 5 May 1983.
[150] *Mathrubhumi*, 22 May 1983.
[151] *Mathrubhumi*, 26 May 1983.

Bible, as well as other religious objects, were placed there. A signboard that read 'St. Thomas Church, Sleeha Nagar, Nilakkal' was installed there.[152] Out of asbestos and iron bars, the church grew. Even as a small hill divided the temple and the church, the cross and the church shed were visible from the temple.

The Nilakkal Action Council moved against this construction. Nilakkal Action Council member, Visala Hindu Sammelan secretary and RSS Pracharak J. Sisupalan said that his people would resist the building of the church 'at any cost'.

On 29 May, Vrindavan Swami led the first demonstration against the church at Nilakkal.[153] A few days later, on 4 June, the agitation took on a more aggressive tone. The Sangh Parivar's network drew men to Nilakkal. Leading sanyasis such as Bhoomananda Theertha, Swami Purushottama Theertha, and Swami Dayananda Theertha joined the fray, making comments about the need to protect Sabarimala.[154] 'Any non-Hindu activity and aggression in the forest region from Plapalli to Sabarimala must be resisted', they said. These men pledged to conduct *tapas*, or ascetic practices, from 4 June at the church.[155] The date was set. The confrontation was to be on 4 June, when a 'protest march of five thousand people was to leave the Sithathodu Harijan Colony for the Nilakkal Mahadeva temple and the Palliyarakavu Devi temple'.[156]

The march took place on 4 June. The police stopped

152 *Kalakaumudi*, 19 June 1983, pp. 6–7; and *Mathrubhumi*, 26 May 1983.

153 *Mathrubhumi*, 30 May 1983.

154 *Mathrubhumi*, 3 June 1983.

155 Ibid.

156 *Mathrubhumi*, 31 May 1983.

the procession and arrested nine swamis as they began their tapas at the church site.[157] Violence was the inevitable result. The police acted by firing at the crowd and arresting a large number. The Nilakkal issue became a national issue, particularly for the RSS and the Sangh Parivar. The national leadership of the RSS passed several key resolutions. Here are some of them:

- ABKM considers as highly reprehensible the acts of the Government such as providing police protection to the trespassers, assaulting the peaceful, revered Sanyasins who entered into the area for doing penance, and beating up and arresting the respectable members of the ladies' delegation to the chief minister at Guruvayur [sic]. It is tragic, that the Kerala Government should have become instrumental in insulting and injuring the three points of Hindu religious honour viz., the Temple, the Sanyasins, and [sic] Motherhood.
- The Government's propaganda tirade against RSS, arrests of more than 3,500 Swayamsevaks and sympathizers, their manhandling and torture in police-lock-ups, police raids, and illegal searches of Sangh Karyalayas, forcible closure of Shakhas at some places, and foisting charges of rousing communal passion and hatred on respectable and peace-loving elders and Swayamsevaks, all these are clearly part of the Government's desperate attempts to make the RSS a scapegoat in order to cover its own sins of commission and omission and to divide the Hindu ranks.

[157] *Mathrubhumi*, 5 June 1983.

- ABKM demands that the Government of Kerala immediately retrace their unjust and oppressive measures against the Hindus and withdraw forthwith all the cases against the Swayamsevaks and others, including many women, and revoke the permission for the church, with a view to restoring peace and harmony in the State.
- ABKM also appeals to the Christians, in general, not to aggravate the situation by making it a prestige issue, and also congratulates the sober elements among them who have openly come out against the present demand for a church at Nilakkal and have exposed the hollowness of the historical and legendary claim over Nilakkal.
- ABKM hereby wishes to caution the Christian brothers and the Kerala Government that if a just and amicable solution is not found without further delay, Hindus all over the country may feel seriously agitated – as they have already begun to feel – about the menace that will be posed to Hindu religious places wherever Christians grow in sizable numbers.[158]

The RSS not only fueled this struggle but defined it. Local claims became national problems, with debates about divinity at the centre of them. Sabarimala went from being a site of heterodox devotion to a flashpoint for the RSS on the issue of Christian influence and 'anti-Hindu sentiment'. Swami Sathyananda Saraswathi, who ran the Nilakkal Action Council, said that the 'Nilakkal issue is an important milestone in the decaying economic and moral Hindu life'.[159]

[158] *RSS Resolves*, pp. 116-117.
[159] *Mathrubhumi*, 6 June 1983.

The Nilakkal Action Council took the initiative further. They decided to hold a Black Day against police action on 7 June across Kerala.[160] The ABAAS was going to hold a special pilgrimage to Sabarimala on 16 July anyway. The pilgrimage was to go on its normal route. But a special group, consisting of thousands, would visit the temple at Nilakkal and conduct a special darsan.[161]

The Church feared the growing wave of anti-Christian sentiment. It began to step back from the attempt to build the church. A conference of Christian religious leaders on 21 July decided that they had no intention of forcibly building a church at the cost of religious fraternity.[162] Sarvodaya leader M.P. Manmadhan offered some proposals for mediation, which were accepted by both the Christian Church Action Council and the Nilakkal Action Council.[163] The first round of discussions that took place in August failed. A new round began on 13 September 1983 at Ranni Perinadu Palace. Pandalam Kerala Varma Raja drew the boundaries of Ayyappa's Poonkavanam, which the Christian leaders accepted. In time, the two Councils found a place in Aangamuzhi, outside what Pandalam Kerala Varma Raja claimed was Ayyappa's Poonkavanam, to build the church.

The RSS then claimed victory in a series of resolutions by its national executive:

- ABKM appreciates and welcomes the efforts of certain

[160] *Kalakaumudi*, 19 June 1983.
[161] *Mathrubhumi*, 15 July 1983.
[162] *Mathrubhumi*, 22 July 1983.
[163] Rajasekharan, 'Ajatha Sathruvaya Kerala Varma Raja', p. 44.

well-meaning social leaders to defuse the explosive situation and see that justice is upheld.

- ABKM hereby heartily congratulates the Hindu populace of Kerala for putting up a united resistance cutting across all political and caste differences.
- ABKM calls upon the Hindu people all over the country to stand solidly behind our Hindu brethren of Kerala. While assuring our Kerala brethren of its humble share in their noble efforts, the RSS also appeals to them to continue to maintain the present spirit of unity so that the integrity and sanctity of the Hindu Dharma and Society will forever remain safe and secure.[164]

The Nilakkal issue had done much damage to the religious harmony in the state. But it provided the Right an issue to cash in. In Kerala, they have always sought to make gains by bringing temples to the heart of their political strategy. This strategy stretches from the Angadipuram Thali temple agitation (1968) to the Thalassery riot (1971), to the Nilakkal agitation (1983), and to the Sabarimala agitation.

PILGRIMAGE TO SABARIMALA

In the journey from an everyday life to a pilgrim's life, a transformation occurs. The 'pilgrim' is transformed, with caste, class, and other social hierarchies disturbed by the pretence of ritual equality. During the pilgrimage to Sabarimala, the pilgrim becomes a swami or an Ayyappan. The idea of the

[164] *RSS Resolves*, p. 116.

'Hindu', without distinctions, enters the journey, although here, new kinds of hierarchies develop, such as the hierarchy of gender. Those who join the pilgrimage participate in the birth of a new kind of collective, a new fraternity that evolves during the walk and then returns with the pilgrim to his home, where he could be drawn into other kinds of religious activity. They become, as Lars Kjaerholm puts it, more concerned about religious life than before as a consequence of their involvement in the Ayyappa and Sabarimala pilgrimage.[165] As he notes:

> It is a plausible hypothesis that strong religious involvement in a cult like that of Ayyappa tends to remind people of other, more traditional aspects of their religious life, and to further their interest in religion in general. Ayyappa devotees tend to be very active in other religious spheres as well. They participate in Bhajans for various other gods, they frequent a great number of local temples, go on pilgrimages to temples, and worship a great variety of gods. Only to very few does Ayyappa worship become so important, that all other gods are neglected. I have found only one devotee of Ayyappa, a guru, who had taken Ayyappa as his *kuladeyvam* and ceased to worship his hereditary *kuladeyvam*, because he declared that now *Ayyappa* was his *kuladeyvam*.

The pilgrimage serves to draw devotees more into an all-encompassing world of religion and transform heterogeneity into homogeneity.

[165] Kjaerholm, 'Aiyanar and Aiyappan Cult in Tamil Nadu', p. 14.

Forty-one Days of Preparation

The Sabarimala temple has emerged as one of the major pilgrim centres in South India. While most other pilgrimages are individual, the Sabarimala pilgrimage or yathra is a collective affair. In places such as Guruvayoor, a devotee can visit and be a pilgrim at any time. But the case of Sabarimala is different. There are fixed periods for the pilgrimage, and the devotee must pass through different stages of the pilgrimage in a systematic and well-ordered manner.

The Sabarimala temple is open for around 120 days a year. The main pilgrimage season lasts for about sixty days, from mid-November to mid-January. The rest of the time, the temple is open to devotees only on the first five days of each Malayalam month. The festival season begins on the first day of the Malayalam month of Vrischikam (from mid-November to mid-December) and lasts for forty-one days. This season is known as *mandala*. The temple is then closed for five days, during which no pooja is conducted. After that, the temple opens for fourteen days culminating in the Makaravilakku festival.

In an earlier time, non-Hindu devotees would join the pilgrimage in relatively large numbers, as reported in the Temple Arson Report (1950), but by the 1980s, the numbers had dropped. An account from that decade offers a sense of the situation:

> I often heard the claim that Muslims and Christians participate in great numbers in the Ayyappa pilgrimage, but although I was constantly on the lookout for them,

I never came across any Muslim or Christian Ayyappa Swamis. Those I have met and interviewed were all Hindus from Tamil Nadu or Kerala.[166]

Part of the reason for this decline could be the sharpening of religious boundaries and the process of homogenization.

Two months before the pilgrimage begins, the devotees who are going to Sabarimala attend a number of devotional gatherings, with bhajans in their heart.[167] The pilgrims go through self-enforced asceticism, such as no sexual intercourse, vegetarianism, and sleeping on the floor. The pilgrimage begins when a guruswami (a veteran of the Sabarimala pilgrimage) gives a neck chain (mala) to the new pilgrim. This chain has to be worn for the entire pilgrimage.[168] Nowadays, the mala is given to the new pilgrim mainly after a Namboothiri priest performs pooja at a temple near the pilgrim's home.

Once the pilgrim receives the necklace, he must live a restricted life. He is supposed to stop shaving, walking barefoot, and abstain from sex, meat, and alcohol. He wears a special Ayyappa pilgrim outfit, a coarse cotton veshti, which is either blue, green, saffron, or black.[169] They become 'swamis', 'incarnations of Ayyappa himself', write Filippo and Caroline Osella. They greet each other with the cry '*Swamiye*' and chant '*Saranam Ayyappa*' ('Ayyappa is my refuge').[170]

Vrischikam (in mid-November), when the Sabarimala

166 Kjaerholm, 'Aiyanar and Aiyappan Cult in Tamil Nadu', p. 8.
167 Ibid., p. 6.
168 Osella and Osella, 'Ayyappan Saranam', p. 733.
169 Kjaerholm, 'Aiyanar and Aiyappan Cult in Tamil Nadu', p. 6.
170 Osella and Osella, 'Ayyappan Saranam', p. 733.

pilgrimage begins, is marked by a flurry of other temple festivals and special poojas, which continue throughout the forty-one-day mandala period. Even temples with no religious activities on their calendars involve themselves in the flurry of activity around the mandala kalam (mandala period). Special arrangements are made for *kettunira* and *malayidal,* two important ritual events. All temples busy themselves with devotional activities, as swamis of various kinds visit as many temples as possible in the forty-one days of the vratha.

Part of the practice of the pilgrimage is creating a sense of *Hindu* identity amongst the pilgrims, not an identity based on region or caste. Earlier, devotees would do the *kettunira* (preparation for the journey) at home, but today it is the local temple that is the main site of preparation, which takes place as a collective religious affair with the participation of all the devotees of the village. This is where gender is a site of complexity. Women between the ages of ten and fifty have been barred from entry into Sabarimala – although legally they may enter since the decision of the five-judge Constitution Bench of the Supreme Court in 2018 – but women devotees participate actively in this initial stage of the pilgrimage. They assemble in large numbers in these temples to observe and participate in the *kettunira.* Gender is set aside momentarily, but asserts itself quickly enough!

During the mandala period, replicas of the Ayyappa temple at Sabarimala are built around the state using banana stumps, bamboo, and coconut fronds. The various idols that are familiar from Sabarimala are placed around these temples and *Ayyappanvilakku rituals* are held. This pooja runs through the night in a specially built mandapam, a hall. In earlier times, the Ayyappanvilakkus were not as extensive as they are now. In parts of Palakkad (southern Malabar) they were largely a ceremony conducted by people from communities such as Nair, Viswakarma, Thiyya, etc. The rituals are still conducted mainly by these people, says Manoj, a *vilakkupattu* artist from Palakkad.[171] The ritual battle between Ayyappa and Vavar in the Ayyappanvilakku is also conducted by people from these communities. The persistence of these customs shows the tentacles of the past that resist the process of homogenization

Ayyappanvilakku used to be a far more modest affair, while increasingly it is celebrated as a big village event associated more with temples. There are huge arrangements and organizational activities behind each such event conducted. It has become a collective festival of Hindus! The Ayyappanvilakku is conducted now for 'collective salvation', for the 'welfare of a collective mass of people'.[172] What was once part of the syncretic culture of the region has now been transformed into a homogenized Hindu tradition.

Journey to Sabarimala

The Sabarimala pilgrimage is meant to culminate after forty-one days at the end of the Makaravilakku festival.[173] That period is extraordinarily busy. Groups of pilgrims – rarely individually – arrive at Sabarimala. According to Osella and

[171] Personal interview with Manoj (Ayyappanvilakku artist), Palakkad, 5 November 2016. Vilakkupattu denotes ritual songs dedicated to Ayyappa, consisting of oral songs related to the Ayyappa legend. These songs are mainly used in the Ayyappanvilakku ritual.

[172] Notices of Ayyappanvilakku at various temples in Palakkad district.

[173] Osella and Osella, 'Ayyappan Saranam', p. 734.

Osella, 'For the pilgrims, as people who are in the guise of renouncers, caste is dead for the forty-one days. The pilgrims mainly come from the middle and oppressed castes. It is also clear that few Dalits participate in this pilgrimage'.[174]

The ritual dynamic to Sabarimala pilgrimage requires some elaboration. It begins at the home of either a pilgrim, at a local temple, or at the home of a guruswami, an older man who has been to Sabarimala for many years, who has shown his devotion to Ayyappa, and who has acquired considerable practical and ritual knowledge of the pilgrimage. In Tamil Nadu, these men are known as *periya swami*. The devotees perform a pooja. This is either done inside a household pooja room or in the courtyard of the home, or inside a temple that has been built for this reason. A lit oil lamp is placed before the image of Ayyappa. The devotees leave offerings (bananas, flowers, puffed rice, and sticks of incense) for Ayyappa. On one side of the image are the offerings, which the pilgrims will take on their journey. The guruswami lights camphor on a plantain leaf to circle in front of the deity after pooja. He then passes the flame to the pilgrims who sit behind him. The Osellas offer a vivid description of the rituals:

> The Guruswami begins to prepare the *Irumudikettu* (literally, two head coverings tied together), filling two cloth pouches (that should be black, white, or red) tied into a single bundle with ritual offerings for Ayyappa and his accompanying deities. The Guruswami begins by pouring clarified butter (ghee) into a number of coconuts,

[174] Ibid., p. 735.

which have been previously bored with one hole and emptied of their liquid; he seals each with a cork. Each pilgrim then receives a number of items to be placed in the *Irumudi*'s two pouches. The main offering to Ayyappa is in the front pouch: one ghee filled coconut together with three handfuls of rice placed there by the pilgrim or by non-pilgrim relatives, an areca nut wrapped in betel leaf, and, for new pilgrims – the Kanni Swamis – a few coins as Dakshina (ritual 'payment'). The rear pouch holds another coconut – whole and not filled with ghee – to be smashed before ascending to the main Ayyappa shrine and a small bag of turmeric powder, some camphor balls, [and] a small bag of white rice. A separate bag contains dried grapes, moulded sugar balls, and bananas to be offered to the god Ganapathi.

With the completion of *Kettunira* the pilgrims are ready to leave. They make the devotional gesture of touching the feet of senior family members, give Dakshina, a few coins wrapped in areca leaf, and receive blessings from non-pilgrim friends and relatives. The Guruswami, standing behind them, balances an *Irumudi* pouch on the head of each pilgrim, who in return touches the guru's feet and offers Dakshina. The pilgrims walk backwards out of the house or Pandal and circle three times around a rock placed at the centre of the courtyard before smashing a coconut on it. They leave without turning to look back.

The pilgrims begin their journey; a circuitous route is followed that takes them to a number of prominent Hindu temples – Guruvayoor, Chottanikkara and Vaikom, for example – before they reach Sabarimala. There are two routes to Sabarimala – a long one and a short one. The long one begins at Erumeli and covers a distance of sixty-five kilometres. Pilgrims follow the mythical footsteps of Ayyappa, then arrive at Pamba *Nadi* (river), where the final ascent to Sannidhanam, Ayyappa's temple, begins. The second route goes directly to the Pamba River. Pilgrims ford the Pamba, then take a bath to purify themselves. They are at the shrine of the elephant-headed Ganapathi, whose shrine marks the start of the journey upwards. The pilgrims go past Appachimedu, Sabaripeedam, and Saramkuthi Aal (a sacred banyan tree at Saramkuthi) before they arrive at the temple.[175]

At Sabarimala, the pilgrims spend time with the three key divinities that are disciples of Ayyappa, Vavarswami, Karuppuswami, and Kaduthaswami. The pilgrims now offer a coconut at the side of the eighteen steps at a tank and then reach Sannidhanam, Ayyappa's temple. They then take their offerings to the other deities inside the temple complex, the Malikappurathamma, in particular, and collect the prasadam.[176] They then retrace their steps, and at the end, they remove the necklace and end the pilgrimage. There is something quite profoundly unifying for the men in the uniformity – the mass of pilgrims who are dressed in the same way, calling each other swami, carrying the same offerings, walking the same route, and following the same rituals. This making of a sacred community is very similar to what Victor Turner defined as *communitas*. In Kerala, there is no parallel

[175] Osella and Osella, 'Ayyappan Saranam', p. 737.
[176] Ibid., p. 738.

to the way in which Sabarimala has become the focal point of the assertion of Hindu masculinity.

In her assessment of the growth of Hindu regeneration movements, historian Uma Chakravarti argues, 'Celibacy is the preferred state for possessing concentrated masculine vigour'. In this kind of chauvinist discourse, she argues, 'masculinity, achieved through renunciate celibacy, is in marked contrast to the Buddhist emphasis on celibacy, which leads to escapism and emasculation'. 'Hindu renunciation,' Chakravarti argues, 'is thus explicitly marked out as an active and aggressive state, which is linked to masculine potency. It distances itself from any negative connotations of passivity because it always holds the promise of resolution and gain – a return to strength and an augmentation of power.' [177] Being a Hindu male practice in general (with the exception of women older than fifty and girls below ten), the Sabarimala pilgrimage is suffused with masculine vigour through the strictest renunciation and mutually reinforced macho abstention. The mood of the pilgrimage has enough scope for everything that Chakravarti suggests is key to the emergence of a Hindu regeneration discourse.

Pilgrimage and Hindu Unity

The ABASS has had an important role to play in the recent history of Sabarimala. ABASS was formed in 1945 in Thiruvananthapuram as a voluntary organization that served

[177] Uma Chakravarti, 'Inventing Saffron History: A Celibate Hero Rescues an Emasculated Nation', in *A Question of Silence?: The Sexual Economies of Modern India*, ed. Mary E. John and Janaki Nair, Zed Books, 2000, p. 256.

the Ayyappa devotees at Sabarimala. At that time, there was no medical facility for the pilgrims. When Dr P.A. Velayudhan Pillai was there that year, a boy fell ill, and he attended to him. After that, Dr Pillai felt that a voluntary organization was needed at the Sabarimala temple. That is why he joined with Achuthan Nair, C.V. Raman Pillai, Krishna Pillai, and P. Subramaniam to conceive the idea for ABASS on 12 January 1945. The men held a meeting at the Sree Chithra Hindu Religious Library in Thiruvananthapuram in April 1945. The first executive committee was formed. It included Justice K.S. Govinda Pillai as the first president, with Dr Pillai as the general secretary, and P. Subramaniam as the treasurer. By 1947, ABASS gave people free medical assistance as well as ginger water (*chukku vellam*) and *annadanam* (donated food). Not long after, ABASS donated the first loudspeaker system for Sabarimala. That year, the Maharaja of Travancore visited Sabarimala. He donated Rs. 700 to ABASS and promised an annual grant of Rs. 8,000. He also gave ABASS land for an office building at the temple complex.[178]

The organization made significant strides in its early years, and in 1948 ABASS moved to expand its reach across Kerala. It first appointed men to expand the reach of the organization and of the Sabarimala pilgrimage across the region – Parmeswaran Pillai (Travancore), Sankara Kurup Sastri (Kollam), K.K. Ilayath (Kottayam) and Raghavan Pillai (Cherthala, Ambalappuzha and Srikrishnapuram). ABASS set up the *Sree Ayyappa* magazine, under the leadership of K.P.

[178] For details on ABASS, visit: http://www.akhilabharathaayyappasevasangamtn.org/ .

Sasthrikal, N.P. Panikar, and Puthezhathu Raman Menon to reach far afield, from Kerala deep into Tamil Nadu.

After the reconstruction of Sabarimala in the aftermath of the fire, the pilgrims began to grow, numbering around four crore according to the latest estimates.[179] It was an incredible expansion. The fire and the campaign around the fire brought ABASS into prominence. That fire gave a fillip to the efforts of groups like ABASS to spread the Ayyappa message and to mobilize people to become devotees across south India. After the fire, a volunteer organization, as *The Hindu* reported it, 'comprising well-trained youth devoted to the task of protecting Hindu culture and religious institutions in the Kerala union has been announced'.[180] The ABASS leadership issued an appeal to all 'Hindu devotees' to 'lead an austere life for seven days from next Saturday', which was 24 June 1950, 'and to proceed to the altar of the deity at Sabarimala for mass worship on the following Saturday'. ABASS, led by P.T. Rajan and Advocate Nagappan Nair, organized an Ayyappa Jyothi, which travelled across Kerala and Tamil Nadu to encourage the rebuilding of the temple and build enthusiasm for the pilgrimage. ABASS thus gave its support to the temple's reconstruction and used the reconstruction as a way to build ties with the public to Sabarimala. In July 1955, ABASS held the World Hindu Conference in Sasthankotta under the leadership of senior IAS official M.K.K. Nair and two disciples of Narayana Guru, Nataraja Guru and Swami Nithya Chaithanya Yathi. People came from about thirty-six nations.

[179] *The Indian Express*, 4 November 2016.

[180] *The Hindu*, 27 June 1950.

P.T. Rajan, an industrialist from Tamil Nadu, played a key role in expanding interest in Sabarimala across his home state. Anthropologist Lars Kjaerholm writes:

> P.T. Rajan is described as a man who worked enthusiastically to spread the worship of Ayyappa in Tamil Nadu. What prompted him to collect money for the new Ayyappa statue at Sabarimala was the fire accident there in which both temple and idol were destroyed. He was a prominent member of the group of people, who collected money from all over Tamil Nadu for the Sabari temple.[181]

Thanks to the efforts of these men, by the 1970s, the Sabarimala pilgrimage had become very popular, and the character of the pilgrimage began to take on a homogenized Hindu form. By the early twenty-first century, ABASS would have 2,570 branches with thousands of members around the world. There are now many associations that bring people together around Sabarimala and simultaneously, into the universe of a homogenous, grand Hinduism, with a section sliding becoming right-wing.

In 1983, during the Nilakkal campaign, ABASS took a leading role. The meetings in which decisions for action to protest against the Church construction were taken, were held in Thiruvananthapuram by the Ramadasa Mission, Chinmaya Mission, Visala Hindu Sammelan, Nair Service Society, VHP, and ABASS.[182]

By 1991, ABASS had the moral authority to drive the

[181] Kjaerholm, 'Aiyanar and Aiyappan Cult in Tamil Nadu', p. 5.
[182] *Mathrubhumi*, 21 April 1983.

agenda related to Sabarimala. When the High Court of Kerala had to decide on the entry of women between the ages of ten and fifty into Sabarimala, the judge prioritized the opinion of the ABASS secretary K.P.S. Nair. The judgment from the Court, which prohibited the entry of women of that age bracket, said:

> That there is a continuous practice of women of a particular age group being prohibited from worshipping in Sabarimala temple has been spoken to by the *Thanthri* of the temple, the President of the Ayyappa Seva Sangham, and a member of the Royal family of Pandalam. These three persons have personal knowledge of the practices followed in the temple for at least half a century.[183]

This shows the moral authority ABASS acquired over the years. The high court took the views of ABASS, the Thanthri, and the Pandalam family as authentic.

ABASS has been officially recognized as an organization that had the authority to provide certificates to prove that one is Hindu. The ABASS certificate is a validated proof for conversion to Hinduism.

Today ABASS has a great deal of influence over the conducting of Ayyappan Vilakku and organizing the Sabarimala pilgrimage. ABASS is one of the most prominent banners under which thousands of Ayyappanvilakku programmes are conducted across the state. It is ABASS that speaks for the pilgrimage and for Hindu unity. Over the years, ABASS has extended its activities to various parts of the world.

[183] S. Mahendran vs The Secretary, TDB. Available here: S. Mahendran vs The Secretary, Travancore ... on 5 April 1991 (indiankanoon.org) .

Through its branches, it organizes activities like spreading the message of Ayyappa bhakti, spreading Hindu consciousness, uniting dispersed Hindus, etc.

Spreading Hindu consciousness, uniting dispersed Hindus, this is the agenda of the hard right, of Hindutva, of the RSS, and its parivar. In the past few decades, ABASS has quite clearly transformed itself from being a volunteer organization. Kerala BJP leader Kummanam Rajasekharan told the RSS magazine *Organiser* in 2006:

> The Ayyappa Unity Movement, an initiative of ABASS and other Ayyappa organizations, proclaims its objective to be 'Hindu' unity through Ayyappa worship and pilgrimage. Ayyappa Unity Movement is for 'protection and strengthening of Hinduism through Ayyappa'. Books on Ayyappa will be distributed to all Hindu houses of Kerala.[184]

In the recent Sabarimala agitation, top ABASS leaders were seen becoming part of the Sabarimala Achara Samrakshana Samithi. There was a dispute within the organization, with some alleging that ABASS national vice president Mohan K. Nair, central working committee member V.K. Rajagopal, and leaders like Mullakkal Sasikumar, N.R.C. Kurup, and Prasad Kuzhikaala violated the organization's bylaws by becoming part of the launch of the Samithi.

[184] Interview with Kummanam Rajasekharan, *Organiser*, 13 August 2006, p. 35.

IN CONCLUSION

The Supreme Court of India pronounced a historical judgment on 28 September 2018. The court was hearing a petition against the restrictions regarding the entry of women into the Sabarimala temple in Kerala. After hearing petitioners from both sides, the five-member constitutional bench proclaimed its verdict allowing the unrestricted entry of women of all ages into Sabarimala. The court reversed the 1991 Kerala high court judgment, which enforced a total ban on the entry of women between the ages of 10 to 50 into this famous temple. This judgment would also invalidate the earlier notifications issued by the TDB regarding the women's entry restrictions.

The crux of the legal battle revolved around the idea of menstruation. The reactionaries argued that the god Ayyappa in Sabarimala is *Naishtika Brahmachari* (Celibate), and historically women of menstruation age don't visit the temple. So, they argued that the restriction is based on religious customs and belongs to the essential practices of religion. The progressives, however, argued that restrictions based on menstruation are unconstitutional and violate women's individual and religious rights and dignity. After hearing both sides, the country's highest court declared that restrictions based on menstrual status couldn't be permitted and allowed unrestricted entry of women into Sabarimala. The 4:1 court decision had wide implications, creating a lot of fallout. A social test would follow.

The judgment contained a powerful indictment against menstrual-based restrictions and discrimination in general. It said, 'The social exclusion of women based on menstrual status is a form of untouchability, which is an anathema to constitutional values'. In the immediate days following the judgment, there was no sign of significant opposition to the judgment in Kerala. But after some days, as the Sabarimala temple was opening for the monthly rituals, opposition to the ruling started to emerge. This opposition came primarily from political forces due to their varied interests and also from revivalist and far-right groups. While the left government in Kerala stood strong in favour of the verdict, many women's rights groups, progressive groups, and other social forces supported the judgement. In the following months, Kerala witnessed a fierce socio-cultural-political battle around the 'issue' of a woman's right to enter Sabarimala.

The Sabarimala struggle against women's entry into the temple showed an unprecedented display by the opposition to a recent Supreme Court judgment in Kerala. Though the opposition seemed and claimed to be against the state government, ultimately, it was directed against the decision of the highest court in the land. When the social might and collective feelings become so powerful to define the extent of judicial reach, the edifice of modernity and its institutions become vulnerable. There were protests and faith-based mobilizations, but also, violent hartals, muzzling of women, threats against voices of reason, and other aggressive actions. Right-wing religious-political interests, upholders of patriarchy, people with communitarian interests, revivalist elements, and political interests all collided. The reactionaries were able to mobilize thousands of religious believers for the 'protection' of the custom.

A counter-mobilization also took place in the state.

This block comprised left and progressive organizations, feminist groups, Dalit groups, tribal groups, etc. The counter mobilization revolved around the idea of *Navodhanam* (Renaissance). These groups saw the mobilization against women's temple entry as a reversal of the values of *Navodhanam* that was an outcome of the sacrifices and great contributions made by the social reformers against various evil practices. Women's mobilizations, cultural activities, and intellectual engagements constituted many aspects of the counter-mobilization. The months-long Sabarimala struggle reached a high point when two women from the age bracket of 10 to 50 entered the temple. However, the atmosphere calmed down after that, and there hasn't been much recent agitation around the issue. The 'issue' is again under judicial consideration as a review petition.

The attention that Sabariamala received also caused renewed interest in the history of this famous temple. There were many claims and counter-claims fought out in the public domain. The history of Sabarimala also became a critical battle terrain. There were many fanciful claims and ahistorical arguments, but factual details also appeared. This book mainly dwelled on the historical transformation of this prominent temple. Though it is challenging to go deeply into the temple's distant past due to a lack of available sources, glimpses of its historical transformation in the contemporary period are outlined in this writing.

The Lord Ayyappa has traditionally been worshipped in Kavus (sacred groves) in Kerala. But we don't have clear evidence regarding the history of the Sabarimala temple from the pre-medieval period. Englishmen have left some information about Sabarimala in their writings. Ward and Conner and William Henry Horsley have written about the temple. Earlier references have not yet become available in detail. So, what we can do is a comparative analysis of the Ayyappa cult with clues from the historical imprints on Sabarimala. Strictly speaking, as scholars like M.N. Srinivasan have pointed out, the Ayyappa cult is historically a south Indian cult. It has been established that there is no mention of Ayyappa in Puranic texts, which otherwise contain a plethora of Hindu gods. Scholar Radhika Sekhar has pointed out that *Bhutanathopakhyanam* from the nineteenth century is the first and only Sanskrit text that narrates the story of Ayyappa in detail. So, Ayyappa, as a local or regional cult, has a lot of credibility.

Back to Sabarimala, also known as Ayyappa, do we have any identifiable, similar gods in history? The most popular and dominant similarity or sameness is with Sastha. Sastha appears in the ancient Puranic texts. But are Ayyappa and Sastha the same? Many have pointed out the iconographic complexities. Sastha is often seen with consorts. But Sabarimala Ayyappa is a celibate god. However, the erstwhile Pandalam Royal family was the custodian of the temple until the Travancore state annexed it. This fact confirms that the Hindu upper castes had been associated with the temple before the eighteenth century. But from what period this had begun and to what extent was their control are questions yet to be answered. The similarity with the Ayyanar god, generally found in Tamil Nadu, is another case in point. Etymological similarities are being pinpointed. One important thing to note is that a lieutenant of Ayyanar, Karuppuswami, is also found in Sabarimala.

The Buddhist antecedence of Sabarimala is tough to prove, though there are several rhetorical claims and attributions. But the connection of the Muslim saint Vavar is historical and established. Also, it is established, that a Christian man was hired to repair the temple after a fire broke out. The tribal claim over Sabarimala is a critical point for consideration. The rights of the Mala Araya community in lighting the Makaravilakku in Poonambalamedu are recognized even by the *Tanthri* (chief priest) family. The temple's location and the importance of the temple god Ayyappa in their socio-religious life point toward a strong tribal familiarity or connection with this god.

The pre-modern history of the temple indicates that it was a temple following heterogeneous traditions. The legacy of Sabarimala in allowing non-Hindus inside the temple reflects this heterogeneous tradition. In the context of Kerala, this is an exception rather than a norm. According to the local tales, Vavar, a Muslim figure who is the close friend or aid of Ayyappa, is also an important constituent of this heterogeneity. The story of Ayyappa's friendship with one Veluthachan (a white-skinned Christian priest) fits well into a syncretic tradition. This syncretism was an essential hallmark of a historical phase. In Kerala, Sabarimala represented and reflected a harmonious spirit, which no other religious space could perhaps match.

But the 1950 Sabarimala Arson case brought significant changes and shifts. The news of the destruction of the idol caused massive protests and hartals also. The expansion of the pilgrimage, with a great flow of believers from other south Indian states, growing popularity in film and other artistic imaginations, increasing vigilance over the possible threats etc., were all a fall out of this incident. The next important chapter was the Nilakkal crucible of 1983. This issue arose over the discovery of a cross and an attempt to establish a church in Nilakkal in the Sabarimala forest region. Protecting Sabariamala became the rallying call, and forging unity by invoking Ayyappa, succeeded in many respects. By this time, the RSS and similar organizations were much more active, and they attempted Hindu mobilization. The Nilakkal issue had communal ramifications.

Compared with other temple pilgrimages in Kerala, the uniqueness of the Sabarimala pilgrimage helps to forge broader Hindu denomination solidarity. The pilgrimage is a collective affair, mostly male affair with some young girls and older women, and forges broader solidarity, unlike any other pilgrimage. The changes related to the temple and the pilgrimage gives Sabarimala more and more of a homogeneous identity. Significant and rapid changes took place in the second half of the twentieth century, especially after the temple fire. This is also reflected in related popular imaginations.

Sabarimala is seen as the heterodox space of divine devotion for a wide range of people and the projected symbol of Kerala's communal harmony. However, homogenization and ecological deterioration of the pristine forest of Ayyappa are happening fast. Perhaps now is the time to see whether its 'historical' self will remain or change.

SELECT BIBLIOGRAPHY

BOOKS/REPORTS

English

Additional Memorandum. *Kerala Floods – 2018*, Government of Kerala, 2018

Alexander, P.C., *Buddhism in Kerala*, The Registrar, Annamalai University, 1949

Clothey, Fred, *Images of Man: Religion and Historical Process in South Asia*, Madras : New Era, 1982.

Clothey, Fred, and A.K. Ramanujan, *The Many Faces of Murukan: The History and Meaning of a South Indian God*, Munshi Manoharlal Publishers, Delhi, 2005

Dubashi, J., *The Road to Ayodhya*, Voice of India, New Delhi, 1992

Goel, S.R., *Hindu Temples: What Happened to Them*, Voice of India, New Delhi, 1998

Goodman, Percival, and Paul Goodman, *Communitas: Means of Livelihood and Ways of Life*, University of Chicago Press, Chicago, 1947

Government of Kerala, *Kerala Post Disaster Needs Assessment: Floods and Landslides – August 2018*, October 2018

Guilmoto, Christophe Z., Sebastian Oliveau, Virginie Chasles, Rémy Delage and Stephanie Vella, 'Mapping Out Social Change in South India. A Geographic Information System and its Applications', *Pondy Papers in Social Sciences*, Institut Français de Pondichéry, 2004

Horsley, William Henry, *Memoir of Travancore, Historical and Statistical*, Govt. Press, Madras, 1839

Iyer, L.A. Krishna, *Travancore Tribes and Castes*, Vol. 1, Govt. Press, Trivandrum, 1937

———, *Travancore Tribes and Castes*, Vol. 2, Govt. Press, Trivandrum, 1939

Jaffrelot, Christophe, *Religion, Caste and Politics in India*, Primus Books, New Delhi, 2010

Jayashankar, S. *Temples of Kerala*, Delhi: COP, 1999

———, 'Temples of Kannoor District' in *Census of India, Special Studies, Kerala*, 1999

John, Mary E., and Janaki Nair (eds.), *A Question of Silence? The Sexual Economies of Modern India*, Zed Books, New Delhi, 2000

Kent, Eliza, and Tazim Kassam (eds.), *Lines in Water: Religious Boundaries in South Asia*, Syracus University Press, USA, 2013

Khan, Dominique-Sila. *Sacred Kerala: A Spiritual Pilgrimage*, New Delhi: Penguin, 2009

Kunjan Pillai, N. *Census of India, 1931. Vol. XXVIII, Travancore*, Trivandrum: The Superintendent, Govt. Press, 1932

Mackenzie, G.T., *Christianity in Travancore*, Govt. Press, Trivandrum, 1901

Mateer, Samuel, *Native life in Travancore*, W.H. Allen & CO., London, 1883

Menon, A. Sreedhara, *A Survey of Kerala History*, Kottayam, DC Books, 2007

Menon, K. Kesava, *Sabarimala Temple Arson Case: Enquiry Report*, Trivandrum: Government of Kerala, 1957

———, 'Pandalam adamanam', Malayalam year 969, in T.K. Velupillai, *Travancore State Manual*, Vol. 2, Appendix

Rao, T.A. Gopinatha., *Elements of Hindu Iconography*, Vol. 2, Part 2, Madras: The Law Printing House, 1916

———, *Travancore Archeological Series*, Vol. 2, Part 2, (Bauddha and Jaina Vestiges in Travancore), Madras, Methodist publishing house, 1910-13

———, *Travancore Archeological Series*, Vol. 2, Part 3, Madras, Methodist publishing house, 1910-13

RSS Resolves: 1950–2007: Resolutions passed by ABPS and ABKM of the RSS from 1950–2007, New Delhi: Suruchi Prakashan, 2007

Sadasivan, S.N., *A Social History of India*, APH Publishing, Delhi, 2000

Sarkar, H., *An Architectural Survey of the Temples of Kerala*, Archaeological Survey of India, New Delhi,1978

Sekar, Radhika. *The Śabarimalai Pilgrimage and Ayyappan Cultus*, Delhi: Motilal Banarsidass Publishers, 1992

Sikand, Yoginder, *Sacred Spaces: Exploring Traditions of Shared Faith in India*, Penguin, New Delhi, 2003

S. Mahendran V. The Secretary, Travancore Devaswom Board, Thiruvananthapuram, AIR 1993 Ker. 42

Sontheimer, Gunther-Dietz, and Hermann Kulke, (eds.), *Hinduism Reconsidered*, Manoharlal Publication, Delhi,2001

Srinivas, M.N., *Religion and Society among the Coorgs of South India*, Bombay: Asia Publishing House, 1952

Thurston, Edgar, and K. Rangachari, *Castes and Tribes of Southern India*, Vol. 4, Govt. Press, Madras, 1909

Turner, Victor, *Dramas, Fields, and Metaphors: Symbolic Action in Human Society*, London: Cornell University Press, 1975

Vaasanthi, *Cut-Outs, Caste, and Cine Stars: The World of Tamil Politics*, Penguin Books, New Delhi, 2006

Van Der Leeuw, G., *Religion in Essence and Manifestation*, Princeton University Press, Princeton, 1986.

Velupillai, T.K., *Travancore State Manual*, Vol. 2, Govt. of Travancore, 1940

Ward, Lt. Benjamin Swain, and Lt. Peter Eyre Conner, *Memoir of the Survey of Travancore and Cochin States*, Vol. 1. Thiruvananthapuram: Kerala Gazetteers Dept., 1994. Reprint, Kerala State Gazetteers Dept., 1863

Ward, B.S. *Memoir of the Survey of Travancore and Cochin 1816-1820*, Govt. Press, Madras, 1891

Malayalam

Bhattathirippadu, Kuzhikkattu Maheswaran, *Kuzhikkattu Pacha – Thanthra Grantham* (Kuzhikkattu Pacha – A Tantric Book) , Panchangam Book Store, Kunnamkulam, 2018

Ganesh, K.N., *Keralathinte Innalekal* (Yesterdays of Kerala),

Thiruvananthapuram: Kerala State Department of Cultural Relations, 1990

Maheswari, S Uma., *Mathilakam Rekhakal* (Mathilakam Records), Kerala Bookstore Publishers, 2018

Nair, Panmana Ramachandran (ed.) *Kerala Samskara Padanangal* (Cultural Studies of Kerala), Kottayam, Current Books, 2011

Namboothiripadu, Chennas Manakkal Narayanan, *Tantrasamuchaya* (Collection of Tantras), University of Travancore, Malayalam Series No. 68, Govt. Press, Trivandrum,1945.

Pillai, Vidwan Kurumallur Narayana, *Sri Bhuthanatha Sarvaswam*, Reprint, Thrissur, Current Books, 1991

Ramachandran, Puthusseri, *Kerala Charithrathinte Adisthana Rekhakal* (Basic Documents of Kerala History), Kerala State Language Institute, Trivandrum, 2007

Ramavariar, Kaikulangara (trans.), *Amarakosham*, Kollam, ST Reddiar & Sons, 1950

Santhikal, Suresh (compiled), *Sarva Namajapangal*, Sharon books, Cherthala,2012

Syamkumar,T.S., *Sabarimala – Hinduthva Tantrangalum Yadarthyavum* (Sabarimala – Hinndutva Tactics and Reality), DC Books, Kottayam, 2019

Vasanthan, S.K., *Nammal Nadanna Vazhikal, Kerala Charithravum Samskaravum* [The Roads We Walked, Kerala's History and Culture], Thrissur: Malayala Padana Gaveshana Kendram, 2011

ARTICLES/BOOK CHAPTERS

English

Bacchetta, Paola, 'Sacred Space in Conflict in India', in *Growth and Change*, Vol. 31, 2000

Brace, C., A. Bailey, and David Harvey, 'Religion, Place and Space: A Framework for Investigating Historical Geography of Religious Identities and Communities' in *Progress in Human Geography*, Vol. 30, 2006

Cashman, Richard, 'The Political Recruitment of God Ganapati', *Indian Economic and Social History Review*, Vol. 7,1970

Chakravarti,Uma, 'Inventing Saffron History: A Celibate Hero Rescues an Emasculated Nation' in Mary. E. John and Janaki Nair (eds.), *A Question of Silence? The Sexual Economies of Modern India, Zed Books*, New Delhi, 2000

Eck. L., Diana, 'India's "Tirthas": "Crossing" in Sacred Geography' in *History of Religions*, Vol. 20, No. 3, 1981

Friedland, Roger and Richard Hecht, 'The Bodies of Nations: A Comparative Study of Religious Violence in Jerusalem and Ayodhya', *History of Religions*, Vol. 38, November, 1998

Gurukkal, Rajan. 'Manufactured legends'. *Frontline*, 1 February 2019

———, 'Yes, Sabarimala is in peril, But not the Way You Think', *Outlook*, 05 November 2018

Kjaerholm, Lars. 'Myth, Pilgrimage and Fascination in the Aiyappa Cult: A View From Field Work in Tamil Nadu', *South Asia Research*, Vol. 2, November 1982

Kumar, Ajit, 'Buddhism in Kerala and its Socio-cultural Ramification', *History Today*, No.19, 2018

Kurian-Findeis, Annakutty V., 'Interfaith Relations in Socio cultural Context of Kerala' in Anindita N. Balslev (ed.), *On World Religions: Diversity, Not Dissention*, Sage, New Delhi,2014

Manoj, Rohan, 'Sabarimala: Restrictions on Women A "Recent Phenomenon"', *Outlook*, 22 October 2018

Mar Gregorios, Paulos, 'Communal Violence in Kerala' (editorial), *Star of the East*, September, 1983

Nair, Sreekala M., 'Facets of Kerala's Religiosity : An Overview', *Introduction to Kerala Studies*, Vol. 1, J.V. Vilanilam, Antony Palackal, Sunny Luke (eds.), IISAC, New Jersey, 2012

Nath, Vijay, 'From "Brahmanism" to "Hinduism": Negotiating the Myth of the Great Tradition', *Social Scientist*, 2001

Osella, Filippo, and Caroline Osella, 'Ayyappan Saranam: Masculinity and the Sabarimala Pilgrimage in Kerala', *The Journal of the Royal Anthropological Institute*, vol. 9, no. 4, 2005

Panikkar, K.N., 'Outsider as Enemy', *Frontline*, vol. 18, Jan 6-19, 2001

———, 'Not Merely a Two-way Contest', *The Hindu*, 7 April 2016

Patnaik, Prabhat, 'Shadow of Fascism', *Frontline*, 12 April 2019

Pillai, V. Narayana, 'Sasta Cult in Travancore: Is it a Relic of Buddhism?', *Proceedings of the Indian History Congress*, Vol. 3, 1939

Prashad, Vijay, '5.5 Million Women Build Their Wall', *CounterPunch*, 14 January 2019

Raja, Rajaraja Varma, 'Some Travancore Dynastic Records (A.D. 544-1677)', *Kerala Society Papers*, First Series, 1928

Sekher, Ajay, 'Pallykanam and Pullykanam:Western Ghats and an EcoCultural Crisis, www.Ajaysekher.net

Shu, Hikosaka, 'Buddhism in Tamil Nadu: A New Perspective', *Institute of Asian Studies*, Chennai, 1989

Srinivas, M.N., 'The Cohesive Role of Sanskritization' in P. Mason (ed.), *India and Ceylon: Unity and Diversity*, Oxford University Press, London,1967

———, 'A Brief Note on Ayyappa, the South Indian deity' in K.M. Kapadia (ed.), *Professor Ghurye Felicitation Volume*, Popular Book Depot, 1954

Thapar, Romila, 'Syndicated Hinduism' in Gunther-Dietz Sontheimer and Hermann Kulke (ed.), *Hinduism Reconsidered*, Manoharlal Publication, Delhi,2001

Turner, Victor,'The Center Out There: Pilgrim's Goal', *History of Religions*, Vol. 12, No. 3, February, 1973

———, 'Pilgrimages as Social Processes' in V. Turner (ed.) *Dramas, Fields, and Metaphors: Symbolic Action in Human Society*, Cornell University Press, London, 1975

Vanita, Ruth. '"Wedding of Two Souls": Same -Sex Marriage and Hindu Traditions', *Journal of Feminist Studies in Religion*, Vol. 20, No. 2, 2004

Ventakaraman,K.R., 'Skanda Cult in South India', *The Cultural Heritage of India*, The Ramkrishna Mission Institute of Culture, Calcutta, 2007

Malayalam

Ganghadaran, Thikkurissi, '*Nanjinatile Kshethra Samskaram*' in Panmana Ramachandran Nair (ed.), Kerala Samskara Padanangal, Current Books, Kottayam, 2011

Iyyankode, '*Ayyappanum Krishnanum*', *Yukthirekha*, September,1983

Jose, A.V., '*Makaravilakku Enna Thattippu*', *Yukthivicharam*, February 1981

Krishnakumar, V., '*Ayyappanum Vavarum Oru Pazhaya Pattu*', *Mathrubhumi Weekly*, vol. xxx1, 26 April1953

Pavanan, '*Prathimasa Rekhakal*', *Yukthirekha*, Vol. 1, September 1983

Pulikkunnel, Joseph, '*Nilakkal Prasnam*', *Yukthivadi Magazine*, Vol. 54, June 1983

Rajasekharan, Kummanam, '*Ajathasathruvaya Kerala Varma Raja*',

Kesari, 11 July, 2010

Sasibhooshan, M.G., '*Aradhanalayangal*', in Panmana Ramachandran Nair (ed.) Kerala Samskara Padanangal, Kottayam, Current Books, 2011

ELECTRONIC SOURCES, WEBSITES, ONLINE MEDIA

Asianet News, https://www.asianetnews.com/

ABASS website, http://www.akhilabharathaayyappasevasangam-tn.org/

BBC, https://www.bbc.com/news

Kaumudi Online, https://keralakaumudi.com/news/

Mathrubhumi English, https://english.mathrubhumi.com/

NDTV, https://www.ndtv.com/

Samayam Malayalam, https://malayalam.samayam.com/

Scroll, https://scroll.in/

The News Minute, https://www.thenewsminute.com/ The Wire, https://thewire.in/

NEWSPAPERS

Deccan Chronicle, 10 October 2018; 14 November 2018

Deccan Herald, Daily, 6 December 2013

Deepika daily, 15 January 1981; 25, 29 March 1983; 11 April 1983

DNA Daily, 30 May 2008

Hindustan Times, 15 February 2019

Kerala Kaumudi Daily, 12, 14, 30 April 1983; 4 May 1983

Malayala Manorama Daily, 10 November 2000

Mathrubhumi daily, 15, 18, 21, 24, 25, 29, 30 April 1983; 4, 5, 9, 10, 16, 22, 26, 30, 31 May 1983; 3, 5, 6 June 1983; 15, 22 July 1983; 17 October 2018; 19 November 2018

The Asian Age, 7 January 2019

The Economic Times, 2, 4 January 2019

The Hindu, 18, 19, 21, 22, 27 June 1950; 2 , 10 July 1950; 10 June 2010; 21, 23, 24 January 2011; 16 January 2012; 14 January 2015; 12 April 2016; 3, 17, 20 October 2018; 1 December 2018; 2 January 2019; 7 March 2019

The Hindu Business Line, 21 June 2005

The Indian Express, 13 October 2018; 1 November 2018; 3 January 2019

The New Indian Express, 29 May 2008; 4 November 2016; 4, 14 October 2018; 14, 16 November 2018; 2, 3 December 2018

The Telegraph, 23 October 2018; 7 November 2018; 4 January 2019

The Times of India, 30 April 2011; 16 October 2015; 7 November 2018

JOURNALS

Economic and Political Weekly, Vol. 6, February, 1998

Growth and Change, Vol. 31, 2000

History of Religions, Vol. 20, No. 3, 1981

Indian Economic and Social History Review, vol. 7,1970

Progress in Human Geography, Vol. 13, 2006

The Journal of the Royal Anthropological Institute, Vol. 9, No. 4, 2005

PERIODICALS

Frontline, Vol. 18, Jan 6-19, 2001
India Today, September, 1983, November 2018; 19 November 2018
Kalakaumudi Weekly, 19 June, 1983
Kesari Magazine, 11 July, 2010
Outlook, 27 October 2018
Star of the East, September 1983
The Week, 5 November 2018
Yukthi Rekha, September,1983
Yuktivicharam Magazine, February 1981

ACKNOWLEDGEMENTS

The September 2018 Supreme Court judgment lifting the ban on women of menstruating age entering the Sabarimala temple, followed by the widespread agitation against women's entry, and the resistance put up by progressive sections of society, invoking the tradition of the Kerala Renaissance, made me feel the necessity of presenting my research on Sabarimala in book form.

I wish to acknowledge with thanks the valuable help and support rendered by a multitude of people. It was Vijay Prashad, Editor, LeftWord Books, who believed in me, and provided invaluable support. I have to thank Dr K.N. Ganesh and Dr K.M. Sheeba who provided historical insights and academic guidance while I was doing academic research on the second part of the book. I should also thank Dr Meera Velayudhan, who has spent her valuable time and intellect writing the preface. Interaction with Professor Romila Thapar was helpful, especially for part two of this book.

I should express special thanks to Sudhanva Deshpande, Nazeef Mollah, and everybody at LeftWord Books for their help in bringing this book out. I must thank all my friends and family members for their valuable support. I am grateful to a web of others, including my classmates and teachers at the University, staff of the various libraries I went to, and colleagues who helped me in various capacities in writing this book. I thank each one of them again. I have put my best effort into preparing this book, and I am solely responsible for whatever shortcomings this book may have.

Jitheesh P.M.